SP

STATE BOARD FOR
TECHNICAL AND
COMPREHENSIVE EDUCATION

The Complete Book of

Weakfishing

South Brunswick and New York: A. S. Barnes and Company

The Complete Book of

Weakfishing

Henry Lyman
Frank Woolner

Library of Congress Catalogue Card Number: 59-8010

A. S. Barnes and Company
Cranbury, New Jersey 08512

Reprint, 1972

Foreword

THERE IS, AMONG THOSE OF US WHO FISH THE TEEMING
American seas, a pleasant tendency to associate any particular sport or game fish with a specific locality and to
carry, forever in our minds, a glorified picture of that fish
superimposed against the spectacular backdrop of its native habitat as we found it, as we knew it—when all the
world was young.

Thus, as surely as pale dawn follows a night of gentle
winds and high stars, the man who has taken his first giant
tuna in the cold and churning seas of Nova Scotia will always associate that blue and silver torpedo with furious
northern waters. Similarly, he who engages in mortal combat with his first big striper at Cuttyhunk; his first tarpon
at Boca Grande; his first bonefish on the air-clear flats of
Islamorada—that man will always couple the fish and the
place.

This being so, we were somewhat shocked, upon level-
ing our typewriters at this foreword, to find that our mul-
titudinous recollections of weakfish and seatrout are not
anchored in any private bays of remembrance. After all,
a man *should* be able to isolate, to localize—to pin down
first impressions and triumphant moments in any phase of

5

salt water angling. Disregarding initial confusion, we decided to do just that.

And we failed. Failed utterly, completely—and were forced to admit as much!

There was a morning at Nayatt Point in Narragansett Bay. The tide turned at nine A.M. and the June sunlight touched a skim of golden pollen on the swelling waters. A mild day. A day of no promise, but one in which it was good to be alive, and warm—and drowsy in a skiff bridled to the current while little, transparent grass shrimp went kicking down the tide in a seemingly hopeless attempt to lure squeteague.

The first squet announced his presence by hitting a big orange and white streamer fly held stationary in the building tide. He hit with that terrific, almost impossible away-we-go surface strike of his kind—and almost took a fly rod into the Deep Six!

That was the beginning of something that a fishing guy never forgets: hundreds of glittering, iridescent squeteague following a chum streak right up to the boat—smashing at shrimp and feather lures, rocketing off to shake free or to wallow on the surface and come to net. Not big squet, but comfortable two pounders—and one that tipped the scale at five. Perhaps that was the beginning.

Perhaps. But we remember cracking the throttle wide open and racing straight into a freshening wind, across a shallow bay at Cape Sable, Florida. Every time the wind gusts caught the bow we swung a little, caught the seas quartering and took gallons of cold, stinging salt water aboard. Don't ever believe that the seas can't be cold in Florida, in March.

We *had* to hurry, for the tide was half down and seatrout were supposed to be congregated over a shell flat east of the Cape. Ed Louys said they were there, and Ed was piling along ahead of us, taking the same beating in another outboard-powered skiff.

We drifted, finally, the wind so strong that each boat canted to leeward while white horses laced the flats—and we cast spin-sized bucktails into water that was practically opaque with the pulverized dust of coral. Each cast brought a sudden, punching strike—and a little seatrout, brought to boat or lost in a moment of flashing action.

We forgot the brine caking on our sunburned faces, the wetness soaking through inadequate waterproofs—and the long trip home. Not one of those seatrout weighed more than two pounds, yet we stood in pitching boats, shouting like maniacs into the screaming wind and fishing as though each cast might seduce the grand-daddy of all trout!

Suspense? Weakfishing offers that, too. Have you ever waded over the flats of Canaveral Harbor in that strange, clamorous hour before dawn when the tide is pouring out to sea and huge trout are waiting for a well-presented lure? That's an experience to challenge Wedgeport in August, or Boca Grande in June! Knee-deep, you take a bearing on a street light across the bay, feel for the drop-off, and inch forward to take your place among a silent group of Cocoa's regulars—all of whom disregard the flapping of big rays in the shallows. Somewhere, out there in the gray, pre-dawn darkness, a button trout is waiting to smash at a slowly retrieved Needlefish.

Or, perhaps your recollections of weakfishing are all tied up in a South Carolina stream when November shrimp flit like pale shadows in the brackish creeks; of garish nights on the Texas coast, with trout popping in the reflection of a gas flare on one of the offshore oil rigs; of wading still flats in the light of a Gulf Coast dawn, fishing a river mouth in Georgia or casting a block tin squid to the big tiderunners of New Jersey's surf.

We've found that weakfishing—call it seatrout fishing if you will—is an engaging game for us, and for millions of sportsmen along the Atlantic and the Gulf coasts. Moreover, we've discovered that the weakie of New York's Peconic Bay is no less a thrill to catch than the seatrout of Florida's Indian River. Whether you seek the common, the spotted, the sand or the silver, this handsome fighter of the flats, the bays and the inlets is always ready to offer battle, no holds barred. Weakfishing is never a local sport, but one that is coastal in application.

In this book we have attempted to collect the loose ends and to present a picture of weakfishing from Massachusetts to Mexico, of the tackle and techniques that take trout. If we can help you to locate the hot spots, to take more fish— or to land one noteworthy speck, we shall be amply repaid for our efforts.

And—we'll see you on the fishing grounds: at Nayatt Point when lilacs are blooming; at Peconic and Great Egg Harbor bays; at Lynnhaven and Charleston and Cocoa; at Biloxi and along the Texas coast. Weakfishermen, from Massachusetts to Mexico, have a habit of getting around!

Henry Lyman
Frank Woolner

Contents

List of Illustrations

11

Metal lures used along the coast.
Fly rod artificials.

(The following illustrations appear as a group following page 96.)

CHAPTER 1

The Fish and Its Habits

WHETTING HIS KNIFE TO A RAZOR EDGE, TRIMMING A STRIP OF squid with the care and art of a sculptor, dreaming the while of silver scales and yellow fins, the weakfisherman stands apart from his saltwater angling companions. The unshaven, wild-eyed face of the striped bass fanatic, the secretive, calculating look common to the snook snatcher, the pent-up fury of the bluefisherman—all these are missing.

Yet when the southwest wind is burdened with an ancient message—that weaks are in at Peconic, that the trout run is on at Lynnhaven, that squet are hitting in Narragansett Bay, that specks have moved into the Indian River, the Homosassa and Biloxi Back Bay—these mild anglers will gather from hundreds of miles distant to be there at the appointed tide. Enthusiasts they may be, but of a gentle sort—more, perhaps, of the true Walton mold. Like the fish they seek, their movements are mysterious, without great fuss and tumult, yet always with a definite purpose.

Also like the fish they seek, their ranks are not of one

13

type alone: but, whether the angler is whipping a long rod along the open stretches of a Jersey beach or flipping a tiny lure on monofilament over a Texas grass flat, the quarry is the same—one of the weakfish family.

This family is not a large one in itself, yet if all the names by which its members are called were placed together, the neophyte might think that an ocean full of different creatures was within casting range. Moreover, each name has its champions among scientists, writers and just plain fishermen.

"Weakfish" is recognized almost everywhere, but many claim it is a misnomer since the species is not weak and presumably was so called because of its soft mouth. (We had to include that valuable bit of information because it is mentioned in every piece of literature on this topic— and who are we to break the chain?)

"Trout" and "seatrout" are the common terms south of the Mason-Dixon line, although in waters further northward the name signifies a sea-run brook trout of an entirely different family. "Squeteague," which is the old Indian name, might be the best general term since it stands apart. Unfortunately, if you say "squeteague" to a Florida angler he will think you are sneezing and will not recognize the word as one applying to sport or food. Add "chickwit," "yellowfin," a dozen abbreviations such as "weak" and "squet," a dozen more modifiers like "spotted," "gray," "speckled" and "bastard" to complete the confusion—and you will see why scientists stick to Latin!

Actually, there are four distinct species of weakfish and all are members of the croaker family, that group which includes such angling favorites as the channel bass, spot, croaker and black drum. Since the varieties of weakfishes overlap in range, one is often mistaken for the other—and

the confusion in common names becomes so acute that it
is best to ignore them completely. Sticking to basic ter-
minology, the four mentioned are: the common (*Cynoscion regalis*), the spotted (*Cynoscion nebulosus*), the silver
(*Cynoscion nothus*), and the sand (*Cynoscion arenarius*).

Starting with the common variety as a basis of comparison from which to discuss the others—just as common in
their own range, incidentally—this member of the tribe
looks very much like its cousins. Slim, moderately streamlined and with no very unusual fin formations, it has the
same general outline as many fresh-water game species of
the trout family.

Coloration varies greatly and evidently depends not only
upon the place where the individual was caught, but also
upon its size. In general, it is greenish-blue above and
white below—with every imaginable shade of purple, gold
and copper in between. The markings on the upper portion of the body, darker than the surrounding skin, are
made up of very short lines rather than of distinct spots.
On large fish, the pectoral and anal fins often are bright
yellow. The body colors are similar to those found in a
light skim of oil floating on the surface of calm water, plus
a few extra shades thrown in for good measure.

Range of this variety is from the Keys of Florida to the
coast of Maine, with an occasional stray wandering as far
north and east as Nova Scotia. However, this species, as is
true of the others, is highly sensitive to cold. Therefore,
for all practical fishing purposes, its northern limit may
be considered to be Cape Cod Bay, Massachusetts. (The
most spectacular evidence of this sensitivity to cold occurred near Beaufort, North Carolina, on November 27,
1903, when a sudden drop in temperature caught thousands of fish in the shallows. They were killed, or stunned,
so that local markets—and gulls—were swiftly glutted.)

Although all four species tend to travel in schools, the size of these groups of common weakfish are usually larger than those of their cousins. Sometimes the massed fish extend for many acres. One particular pod, back in 1881, caused even the sedate *New York Times* to carry headlines.

"A GREAT CATCH OF FISH—WHAT THREE SMACKS CAUGHT OFF ROCKAWAY," the story was titled. Three menhaden boats seined 200,000 pounds of weakfish in a short time and, according to a boat crew member, "the water was red with fish, but they didn't break the surface as menhaden always do." The attempts of the boat operators to dispose of their catch is a story in itself. One, whose skipper quarrelled with the Fulton Market dealers, tied up at the foot of Beekman Street. Let the *Times* take it from there:

"A crowd speedily gathered about the boat, and the fish sold almost as fast as they could be handled at 25 cents a pair. The pressure of the crowd became so great at one time that police assistance was invoked and Officer William Brown, of the steamboat squad, was detailed to stay on the boat. While Owen (the seller) was selling the fish at 25 cents a pair, an attempt to break the price was made by two well-known longshore characters, Jack Sullivan, the shark-catcher, and T. Long, alias 'Blindy,' who bought one thousand pounds of the fish at one cent per pound, and stood on the street retailing them at 20 cents per pair."

Unfortunately, we have never been able to discover further details concerning the price breaker with the fascinating occupation, nor concerning his companion—who obviously was not as lacking in sight as his name would indicate. However, from this rather long-winded illustration, it can be seen that common weakfish travel at times in schools of extraordinary size. For those interested, we might mention that the size of the weaks in that 200,000 pound catch ran between seven and three pounds apiece.

As far as size in general is concerned, the common weakfish is said to reach a weight of thirty pounds, but authorities apparently are unable to produce verified records to support this statement. A 15-pounder is a rare fish and the 17-pound, 8-ounce specimen taken by A. Weisbecker, Jr., off the Mullica River in New Jersey on September 30, 1944, has stood for many years as the rod and reel record. "School weaks" are usually considered to be anything under two pounds: when they hit the four pound mark, they are often classified as "tiderunners."

Although there is variation among individual specimens, a one-pound fish measures about 15 inches; a two-pounder, about 19 inches; a five-pounder, about 26 inches, and a 10-pound catch, about 31 inches. In other words the weakfish, like most gamesters of the ocean, becomes chunkier and deeper in proportion to its length as age increases.

Rate of growth is comparatively slow—about two to three inches a year after attaining a length of eight inches in the first season. Maturity is not reached until the species is almost three years old.

Despite the fact that the weak grows slowly, it feeds well and often. Although not as voracious as the bluefish, it rarely lets an opportunity of taking a meal pass by—which is one of the reasons why it is a popular coastal sport variety. Favorite food of the youngsters are shrimp, tiny mollusks, crustaceans and worms of all kinds. As the species grows larger, bait fish of all types, squid and crabs are added to the menu. The angler would do well to remember that, no matter what its age, weakfish never seem to lose their specialized taste for shrimp—even though shrimp may no longer comprise the bulk of diet.

Unlike humans, the female of the species makes no noise at all—while the male is notably vocal, and can set up quite a fuss with its croaking. This croaking occurs both in and out of water, and some observers report that weakfish, particularly the spotted variety, make such a noise under water that the sound is distinctly audible through the hull of a boat. While we have never heard this chorus ourselves, evidence of it comes from such authoritative sources that it cannot be ignored. Undoubtedly this characteristic of the fish has given rise to the many tall tales concerning bamboo reed calls which are supposedly sounded underwater, by anglers, to attract their quarry. There is also the technique of harnessing a vocal pigfish to decoy weakies—but more of that later.

Disregarding the fish calls, sound made by anglers still has a considerable effect among these fish. A surfaced school of common weaks will vanish as though by magic if an oar is accidentally bumped against the side of a boat or if an anchor is hurled overboard with a great splash. All of the four weakfish species are repelled by foreign noises of this kind, but the southern varieties are attracted by noises that simulate frantic bait; they'll rise from the depths to take a lure if a commotion is caused on the sea's surface. Undoubtedly this seeming contradiction in behavior is due in part to the character of the waters and bottom over which fishing is taking place.

Since readers of this volume presumably are more interested in catching weakfish with hook and line than they are with the biology of the species, we will skim lightly over the sex life of the fish. Suffice it to say that spawning apparently occurs from May to October and the period from mid-May to mid-June is the peak for the common variety. This spawning activity usually takes place at night, near the mouths of large estuaries.

Those who think the world is topsy-turvy will be in full agreement with a newly hatched weakfish. The fry swim upside down when first hatched because an oil droplet, which gives the egg buoyancy, is not absorbed for several days. Once it has been absorbed, the fishlet swims normally for the remainder of its days.

Common weakfish can be divided into two races—and possibly more than two. Distinct groups consist of fish which spawn south of Cape May, New Jersey, and those which spawn north of that point. It is interesting to note that at least half, and perhaps as much as three-quarters, of the supply of weakies in the Long Island, New York, area apparently are hatched in Chesapeake Bay. Therefore, intensive fishing for the species in the Chesapeake may have a very marked effect upon the supply in Peconic Bay and surrounding waters.

Despite the fact that brackish waters, such as those of the Chesapeake, are among the favorite haunts of the northern species, all the authorities we have consulted— and our own experience—indicate that the fish never run into purely fresh water. Genio Scott, writing in 1875 in his "Fishing American Waters," stated flatly that the species "never visits fresh water." Scott also made the fascinating observation: "It's eye being oval, it is supposed to possess the strongest sight of any estuary fish." We agree with the first remark, but withhold judgement on the last until eye charts for underwater use have been perfected.

Spotted weakfish apparently run further into fresh waters than their common cousins. Although they cannot survive for long in water of little salinity, there is a possibility that they move across the dividing line from time to time in coastal rivers. An interesting experiment in Texas revealed that transplanted seatrout would not live in a fresh water lake, but would live in Lake Kemp, an impoundment of the Big Wichita River, which has a high salt content.*

Henry B. Bigelow and William C. Schroeder, in the second edition of the classic *Fishes of the Gulf of Maine*, published in 1953, elaborate upon the coastal movements of the common weakfish: "They are usually found in shallow water along open, sandy shores and in the larger bays and estuaries, including salt marsh creeks. They even run up into river mouths, but never into fresh water so far as we know." Other authorities make similar comments, which have yet to be disapproved. And, to cap the measure, we have on several occasions surreptitiously tasted the waters of Florida coastal rivers from which we have just hauled spotted seatrout. On every occasion, even though we were angling at some distance from the sea, the water was brackish.

Before leaving the common weakfish and branching forth on its relatives, it should be noted that cycles of abundance and scarcity have been very pronounced over the years—far more so than in the cases of the other three. There is—and mark this well—no definite pattern in these cycles; the fundamental causes of them have not been determined. Some claim that weaks are plentiful when bluefish are scarce, and *vice versa;* others say that the controlling factor is the supply of menhaden or other bait fish. The only definite conclusion is—that nobody knows. So little research has been done that no one can make a state-

* Gordon Gunter of the Gulf Coast Research Laboratory in Mississippi has reported that small specimens of spotted weakfish have been taken in quantity from waters of salinities as low as 2.3 parts per thousands—virtually fresh water. This report reached our desk just as this volume was going to press and establishes beyond question the fact that the smaller fish definitely cross the dividing line between brackish and salt waters.

ment on the subject with any appreciable number of facts to back a theory.

As an example of the leaps and dips in weakfish supply, look at the historical record. From New York to Boston, the species was plentiful at the end of the 18th century. Weaks then became so scarce that one, caught off Provincetown, Massachusetts, in June of 1838, was sent to Boston for identification—because no fisherman knew what it might have been. Slowly, thereafter, the supply increased and, from 1901 through 1904, fishing was the best in the history of the new world.

Another decline then set in and, by 1910, few were being taken. The fish began to make a comeback in 1921 and increased rather steadily in numbers until 1949, when an abrupt slump occurred. Part of the cause of this may have been an increase in the intensity of the commercial fishery in Chesapeake waters. In more recent years there has been a slight gain throughout the northeastern section in such hot spots as Peconic Bay on Long Island, New York, but the catches in 1957 and 1958 could not compare to those of the 1901-04 era.

Captain "Chicken John" Boschler of Bay Shore, Long Island, New York, is undoubtedly one of the most celebrated weakfishermen on the Atlantic coast, dedicated to angling for the species above all others. His records of the ups and downs of the supply are interesting. In his journal of trips aboard his boat *Doris,* entries are accurate and complete.

According to these figures, catches made in Peconic and Great South Bay from this one boat were as follows: 1934, 1,223 large weakies; 1938, 6,698; 1939, a drop to 1,496; 1946, a jump back to 8,660, and an all time high of 10,121 in 1947. In 1955, the catch was the poorest of all, a slim 650 fish. A total of 1,457 was reached in 1956 and approximately 2,000 in 1957. As this is written, it looks as though the 1958 total would be even higher—an encouraging sign for the future.

Cooperative management of this fishery among eastern seaboard states might well increase the supply for all concerned and, as this is written, such management is well along in planning stages. It should be noted that, no matter how low the supply seems to fall, there always seem to be a few tiderunners—big fish which travel singly or in very small schools—caught at scattered spots along the coast.

Fortunately for the angler in more southern waters, the violent ups and downs in the supply of spotted or speckled seatrout are not so noticeable. This member of the family is very similar to the common variety in general outline, although it might be considered a trifle more streamlined.

Coloration cannot be considered a definite identifying characteristic, despite the fact that some writers wax lyrical over the beauties of the southern species when compared to its cousins. We have seen specimens taken from widely separated fishing grounds on which the color of the skin of both common and spotted has been almost identical. However, there is one sure way to tell the two apart: the spotted has round, almost black, spots on both the dorsal and caudal (tail) fins. The round spots on the upper part of the body are also obvious, but sometimes are confused with the short, dark lines on the body of the common variety. Remember the marked fins and you will never have trouble in identification.

In general, the speckled species is found in more shallow water than the common, all other conditions being equal. The exceptions may be numerous, but this may still be considered a rule of sorts. Another fact which may be classified along similar lines is that the common weak favors hard bottom over which to feed while the spotted is often found over soft mud or mucky grass beds.

Although the world record spotted seatrout taken by rod and reel was smaller by more than two pounds than the record common, this cannot be considered a fair picture of the situation. As this is written, a 15-pound, 3-ounce fish, caught by C. W. Hubbard at Fort Pierce, Florida, on January 13, 1949, holds top position. However, the Cocoa, Florida, region annually boasts several specimens in the 12-pound class. No such reports of common weaks are made.

Undoubtedly the general statement by scientists that the common species grows larger than the spotted is true. In recent times, however, the size records tip the scales in favor of the spotted. There is an authenticated record of a speck of sixteen pounds, but this was a giant of the clan. Eight to eleven-pounders are not uncommon, while the average taken by anglers all along the coast ranges somewhere between the one and three-pound marks. In waters of the western part of the Gulf of Mexico, a three-pounder is considered a big fish.

One interesting point brought out by a study being conducted by the Marine Laboratory, University of Miami, is that there evidently occurs a high mortality among male spotted seatrout after their third year of life. Almost all four year old and over specimens were found to be females. Anglers have evidently realized this for some time and have called large fish "sow trout." (At Cocoa, Florida, any fish weighing more than six pounds is called a "button trout," because it is eligible to win an honorable mention button in the annual *Field & Stream* fishing contest.)

Little was known of the life cycle of the species until this study by the Marine Laboratory had been undertaken, but the following facts have now been confirmed. First, growth of the fish appears to be rapid during its first year of life, during which an average length of six to seven inches is attained. Growth from that time on is evidently fairly constant, at least in Florida waters.

Second, spawning evidently takes place in the spring with the peak during mid-May and early June. There is some variation in the exact times of spawning, depending upon the geographical location which probably causes a difference in water temperatures. Thus, spawning in Cocoa is about three weeks later than spawning in Biscayne Bay. Eggs, in all cases, are dropped in fairly deep water.

Finally, there appear to be both resident and migrant populations of fish in Florida waters. To just what extent these two populations intermingle, whether or not they interbreed, and whether or not the migrations are an annual affair have yet to be determined.

The range of this species is far wider than that of any other of the clan. Strays have been taken as far north as New York, but it is not until Maryland is reached that they are abundant. From Chesapeake Bay southwards to Florida's Keys, they are an angling favorite. Specks also provide sport all along the Gulf shores through Alabama, Mississippi, Louisiana and Texas—even into Mexico below Tampico. According to Miss Francesca LaMonte of the American Museum of Natural History, they are found as well in the Gulf of California during winter and spring.

As is true of most marine species, spotted weakfish tend to travel in schools when young. These schools, although not as large in numbers as those made up by common weakfish, often will cover the greater part of a grass flat and, under such conditions, are easily caught by commercial and sport fishermen. The older and larger "sow trout" travel for the most part either singly or in very small groups. When the fish become large they tend to seek

larger bait fish for food, as might be expected. Huge
shrimp then replace the grass shrimp in their diet, and
big minnows and mullet take over from the smaller stuff.

Highly sensitive to cold, spotted seatrout will head for
deep holes the moment there is any indication of a drop
in water temperatures. At this time, even the big old soak-
ers may travel together in considerable numbers. Under
normal circumstances, they tend to lead a solitary life,
hanging in the deep holes and channels during daylight
hours and moving onto the grass flats after sundown.
There, the natural foods may be anything from mollusks
to marine worms, from squid to shrimp—and never forget
those shrimp.

Shrimp are also favored by the silver seatrout, a small
member of the family which is found from Maryland to
Texas and is especially popular as a sport fish in Gulf waters. Rarely will one of these little fighters reach the
weight of three pounds and the greatest number caught
weigh less than one pound. More chunkily built than the
other species, coloration on this fish, as the name suggests,
is lighter than that of the common and spotted varieties.
Spots are lacking and the main distinguishing feature is
the rounded tail.

Virtually nothing is known about the life cycle of the
silver or white seatrout. It ranges in waters between three
and ten fathoms deep, feeds on the ever popular shrimp
to a large degree and is sought primarily in Gulf waters
where it is present throughout the year. Best fishing is had
from October to May, during which time the little silver
comes close to shore. When the heat of summer is at a peak,
it moves into deeper waters.

Often confused with the silver seatrout is the sand
trout. The two are so much alike that a count of anal fin
rays or spinal vertebrae is the only sure method of distin-

guishing one from the other. The silver, *Cynoscion no-thus,* has eight or nine rays and 27 vertebrae while the sand, *Cynoscion arenarius,* has 11 rays and 25 vertebrae. Sportsmen rarely care—they happily catch either species.

The sand seatrout, according to Louis Rene Rivas of the Marine Laboratory at the University of Miami, is found only in Gulf waters, while the silver shows up in the Atlantic off Florida from time to time. When it comes to the comparative size of the two species, there is some disagreement among the authorities. Those who have observed the two, primarily in Florida waters, say that the silver seatrout is the midget of the clan—while those who hail from Texas state flatly that the sand trout runs smaller on the average. Whoever is right—and probably both groups are right in their own bailiwicks—they are arguing about very small weights in the first place. A three pounder of either species is a monster; the usual catch weighs less than a pound.

Comparison of the habits of the two is largely a comparison of localities where the fish are found. The sand trout frequents much more shallow waters than its cousin. In the shoal bays and sounds along the Gulf, it can be found through the winter months—although angling is best in the fall. As waters warm, fish head for deeper and cooler surroundings. Their favorite food? Again—our old friend, the shrimp.

Pinpointing the best time of year for silver and sand seatrout fishing is not difficult because conditions in the greater part of their range are fairly constant—hot summers, which drive fish to deeper water, and cooler winters, which bring them back within reach of the small boat and shore caster.

To be anywhere near as exact concerning the common weakfish and its spotted relative is difficult. Differences in climate and coastal formations serve to complicate matters. Throw in a migrational pattern that no one has analyzed— or even determined—and the picture becomes a trifle confused.

In general, from Cape Cod to the Virginia Capes, the first real run of common weaks is underway by mid-May with the peak in June. There are local variations caused by weather conditions, but the old saying that fish appear when the lilacs start to bloom is a fairly sound one. At the entrance to Chesapeake Bay itself and in the lower reaches of that body of water, fishing starts almost a full month earlier—but note that Virginia and Maryland lilacs are going strong at that time.

As is true in the case of many saltwater sport species, first fish to arrive in a given area are usually swimming and feeding deep. As water temperatures rise, weakfish find their meals closer to shore and nearer the surface. During the summer they are rarely found at depths greater than forty feet.

Theories on migrations of this species are numerous, yet the only one that has been substantiated to any great degree is that concerning the movement of weaks from the Chesapeake to Peconic Bay in New York. Along the rest of the coast they seem to play a sort of marine game of musical chairs. Fish which have wintered near Florida apparently move up to the Carolinas to replace those which have wintered in that neighborhood and, at the moment, are heading for Virginia. So it goes all along the coastline and, until more research is done, the best we can do is guess the complicated movements of the various schools.

However, north of the Virginia Capes after mid-May, angling for the common weak improves in almost direct relationship to the thermometer reading. In southern New England, fishing reaches a peak in June and early July, slacks somewhat during August and improves, especially for larger fish, in September. New York and New Jersey fishing follows the same general pattern, except that early summer catches are better than those further north. The fall run, which usually supplies the larger fish, may continue until November.

In Delaware and coastal Maryland, the spring and fall runs are most important. During the hot summer months, many fish either seek deep water or head further north. Catches follow much the same pattern within the confines of Chesapeake Bay, with the season extended from mid-April through, sometimes, the entire month of November. As elsewhere in its range, the fall trout is likely to be near the surface, where it pleases sport fishermen.

Ranges of the common weakfish and the spotted variety begin to overlap in the Chesapeake and anglers take mixed catches. By the time the Carolinas are reached, the speckled trout is the favorite. Moreover, from this area southward, the speck becomes one of the most popular saltwater sport and food varieties.

Here, again, fall and spring runs are best—a fact which is true along the entire Atlantic range of this fighter. Big schools of fish apparently move offshore during cold weather, although some are always to be found in deep channels and holes inshore. In midsummer, when the sun is high, look for speckled trout in deep water. Night fishing may provide an unexpected bonanza during the greatest heat of the season.

As far as the spotted seatrout is concerned, there is little question that it is a favorite among anglers throughout its range. Fairly plentiful, reasonably easy to catch and present in a great many areas, it wages a creditable battle on light tackle. From northern Florida to the Chesapeake, the same general pattern of migration must be taken into account: inshore and northward as the weather warms, offshore and southward as it cools.

As the Florida line is approached, more and more fish will be found wintering in deep cuts, tidal creeks and holes. During cold snaps, these specks are comparatively inactive, while a warm spell will put them on the feed. During these periods of relative abundance, an angler with local knowledge can do well with deep-running artificials or with live bait drifted near the bottom. (As has been previously noted, the species is highly sensitive to temperature change. A ten degree drop in the thermometer can ruin fishing in short order. It is well to keep this in mind when planning a trip.)

The spotted trout reaches a peak of popularity as a rod and reel fish in Florida waters and in the Gulf of Mexico. Present almost everywhere throughout most of the year, it can be taken by anglers from all walks of life, regardless of their financial status. If a man can walk, drive or fly to the nearest bridge, pier, rowboat or channel bank, he will have a perfectly good chance to catch his quota.

Along the east coast, in the area extending from Florida's Cape Canaveral southwards and around into the Gulf of Mexico, fish remain active through the entire angling season—January to January. On the Gulf Coast itself, trout are the backbone of the sport fishery: at river mouths, in the tidal sections of the rivers, in bays and estuaries, on the grass flats—everywhere they swim—the specks are sought by rod and reel anglers. These trout may not grow as large as they do on the Atlantic side, but they remain favorites.

For large fish, there is little question that the huge, sheltered Indian River section, which runs from Allenhurst right down to St. Lucie Inlet, year after year produces the spectacular catches. At times, in areas such as those surrounding Cocoa and in the Banana River section, spotted trout are fished to the exclusion of all other species. The reason is obvious: they are plentiful and chances of taking a really big fish are above average.

Even in the areas where it is resident, however, spotted seatrout follow a definite migratory pattern of sorts. Not only do they move along the coast, but they move from deep water to the grass flats in warm weather and then back to the depths if the temperature becomes too hot or too cold. Actually, the migrations north and south make comparatively little difference in the Florida supply, for "replacement" fish are migrating, in their turn, to fill the vacancies.

Draw a line from Corpus Christi, Texas, to St. Petersburg, Florida, across the Gulf of Mexico and you will have a rough division of waters in which the speckled trout seasons change. North of such a line, the best angling occurs between October and May. South of it, especially along the Mexican and Texas shores, more catches are made during June and July. It is quite possible that the seatrout which follow this migratory pattern are a different race than those commonly found on the Florida Gulf shore, although they definitely are of the same species. One thing is certain: western fish run small and a two-pounder is a large specimen.

Both silver and sand seatrout follow the same general movement as their northwest spotted cousins. The sand variety, since it feeds in very shallow water, is apt to move offshore a little before the silver species when the summer sun is high.

Movements of the weakfish family are all-important to the angler, but behavior of the fish themselves during these movements is even more important. As noted, first comers to any given area are usually found in deeper wa-

ter than they will choose later in the season. Both water
temperatures and food are contributing causes. Another
thing that should be considered are the creatures that feed
on the trout.

Predators of all kinds haunt the weakfish from the time
it is an egg until its death. A school of bluefish, for example, will drive weaks before them and leave blood and
destruction behind. Gulls gorge on any unfortunate specimens made logy by cold water. Even their own fry must
move out of range of the jaws of cannibalistic parents.
Thus, it may be that a migration starting through one
particular area will be scattered and re-routed simply because those enemies which feed upon the weakfish are too
numerous.

Such active enemies are not alone in their destruction.
There are countless parasites which chew, burrow, suck
and munch on weakfish from both within and without. As
far as the angler is concerned, most of these may be ignored unless, as is sometimes the case, a body worm infests
a fish to the extent that it is lean and highly unappetizing
on the table.

One external parasite should be noted, since its presence often changes the behavior of the fish. This is a
type of sea louse, known locally as a tick in many areas.
The small creature can be seen clinging to the fish,
particularly around the belly and vent. When seatrout
are infested with these insects, they become angry with
the world and will sulk. Rarely will they hit a bait or
lure. When the summer sun gains strength, the lice apparently leave their hosts and the fish are lively once more.
Certain areas have more of these lice than others, but
they may be found almost anywhere, particularly during
the early season.

With overlaps, with range, with migratory patterns confused, with the identifications of the various species often incorrect, it is little wonder that exact locations of the various fishing grounds cannot always be given in detail. Fortunately, there are enough of these spots so that a majority of anglers may be assured of a fair shake. What to look for, when to fish, and what to use in the fishing will be the topics covered in this book.

CHAPTER 2

Basic Tackle

IF, TWENTY YEARS AGO, WEAKFISHERMEN OF THE ATLANTIC and Gulf coasts had been asked to name their favorite tackle combinations, the vote would have indicated confidence in a variety of outfits but would have ignored the one rig—spinning—that today reigns supreme.

Prior to World War II, coastal anglers used everything from fly rods to high surf sticks on weakfish, but few employed threadline tackle. Progressing in a southerly direction, from the northern boundary of the fish's range in Massachusetts to the Gulf of Mexico, the following rigs were deemed important: in the far north, pre-war purists liked a fly rod for work in a chum streak, a plug casting outfit similar to that used on inland black bass for use with artificial lures, and a light squidding combination for those occasions when big tiderunners ventured into the surf.

From southern New Jersey, through the Carolinas to Florida and the Gulf, sport fishermen accorded top honors to the plug casting outfit and the popping rod—which was,

33

and is, a sort of hybrid surf and light plugging combination. Florida anglers, particularly those engaged in fishing for the market, also employed cane poles and short lengths of stout, linen line. (You may still see an occasional seatrout fisherman of the old school, rowing slowly and philosophically over a southern grass flat with a half-dozen cane poles jutting, left and right, from the gunwales of his craft.)

Quite naturally, a certain percentage of boat fishermen have always used light boat rods and bay reels for trolling and drifting. Note, however, that the tackle employed in trolling is unlike that chosen for hard-mouthed gamesters. A limber, delicate stick designed to fight a weakfish without tearing the hook out of that species' paper-thin mouth is required.

All of the foregoing tackle combinations are still in use along the coast, and several are of considerable importance. Nonetheless, the man who loads for seatrout in this atomic age should regard one outfit as close to indispensable. In weakfishing, spinning deserves a majority vote of confidence.

Threadline gear is ideally suited to this sport—so classically made to order that a single, well-chosen outfit may be adequate from Massachusetts to the Gulf of Mexico and for fish ranging in size from the little sand trout of the Gulf to the big yellowfin tiderunner of Long Island. The great virtue of the spinning outfit in this work, even more important than ease in casting, is the resilience of the rod and the benefits of monofilament line working against a smooth, light drag.

The finest all-around seatrout fishing combination in action today would include a light and limber glass rod of approximately six to seven feet overall length and calibrated to flip lures or baits in the one-half to one ounce class, a small to medium sized spinning reel loaded with six pound test monofilament line, and an assortment of bucktails, plugs and spoons. Live baits may be used with spinning gear and the outfit may be put to profitable employment in trolling or live-lining a chum streak.

Basically, the fresh water spinning rig is adequate and will take the heaviest weakfish now swimming in Atlantic waters. Note, however, that fresh water gear is seldom designed to resist salt water corrosion. Therefore, if you choose to employ the inland rig, be sure to rinse it in sweet water at day's end.

Similarly, while an outfit which ideally handles one hundred yards of six-pound test line is sufficiently heavy to whip a big seatrout, thousands of anglers prefer a heavier test. This, of course, is insurance against disastrous meetings with larger saltwater battlers which often invade the seatrout stamping grounds.

In Florida, for example, the standard spinning outfit employs eight pound test monofilament, and the rod usually measures eight feet from butt to tiptop. This combination is hardly balanced, in northern eyes, yet it is a proven one. Southern sport fishermen use it to hook and land everything from seatrout to big tarpon—and you can't argue with success.

It is nonetheless true that anglers who specialize in catching the huge seatrout of the Indian River section, from Cape Canaveral south to Ft. Pierce and the St. Lucie River on the east coast of Florida, most often employ light gear. Even the rod and line commercial fishermen—and there are plenty of them in operation around Cocoa, which has been called "Trout Fishing Capitol of the World,"—use six-pound test monofilament and find it adequate.

Selection of an ideal spinning combination for use on

weakfish thus boils down to personal preference and, perhaps, a question: will the outfit be used on other species? If the answer is in the affirmative, better invest in the medium weight stick which will handle eight-pound test line.

While many spinning enthusiasts will insist that no other tackle combination has any business on the weakfishing front, there is a definite place for all of the various outfits. Thousands of anglers cut their trout fishing teeth on the popping rod and service reel; other thousands are just as well acquainted with plug casting and squidding outfits. Trollers and drift fisherman employ their own versions of boat tackle, and there is a sizeable group dedicated to angling with a fly rod. Finally, in all of the Atlantic states south of New Jersey, and in the Gulf of Mexico, an army of cane pole mechanics take astronomical numbers of trout.

It has always been our considered opinion that the worth of any outfit must be judged by its success on the field of action and, equally important, by the degree of sport it offers in achieving that success. Quite naturally, there is a delicate balance of requirements involved—but the fact remains: ideal gear must insure somewhat equal helpings of excitement *and* fish in the basket at day's end.

With the possible exception of the cane pole (even this is debatable), all of the tackle combinations that have come to be accepted as weakfish weapons are effective—and sporting. The cane pole man may want fish more than he wants thrills, but even that worthy registers excitement when a big speck comes blasting out of the grass flats to investigate a popping cork beneath which is suspended a fresh shrimp.

Moreover, each tackle combination is well chosen for a specific task. Take, for example, the orthodox bait casting

rig which is as all-American as the hot dog—and just as
popular throughout the length and the breadth of the
nation. In the hands of an accomplished caster, the plug
rod and multiplying reel achieves as much distance as its
threadline counterpart and is better suited to lure control.
Plug casters enjoy a mastery over surface popping or
splashing baits that is denied to the spinner—who is usually pre-occupied with the prevention of loose line on the
spool when he is popping a top-water lure.

On the debit side of the ledger, plug casting is a game
reserved for the somewhat expert angler. The statement
that distance in casting is comparable to that achieved by
spinners must always be qualified. The beginner at spinning will definitely cast further than the beginner at plug
casting. Similarly, an expert plugger achieves more control
of line and lure when casting in a brisk wind, but the
amateur is at a complete loss and would be better able
to fish with spinning tackle. Finally, the average plug
casting reel is a "fixed gear" instrument and lacks a
smoothly operating drag. The absence of such a drag,
especially when the angler applies too much butt pressure
on a running fish, often rips the hooks out of a weakie's
tender mouth.

This particular handicap of bait casting has been reme-
died by several manufacturers who have installed star
drags on their standard bait casting reels. Moreover, the
latest designs permit the use of monofilament on revolving
spool models marketed by most of the big firms. No one,
however, has yet devised a quadruple multiplying reel
that can be mastered (well enough to employ on the
fishing grounds) within a half hour of practice and in-
struction. This is one selling feature of the spinning reel.

Do not, however, assume that bait casting will soon be
a lost art; thousands of coastal anglers, and particularly

the seatrout fishing regulars of the Deep South, will continue to use this combination so long as it proves ideal for day-in, day-out casting and "Florida Whip" retrieves on the offshore grass flats.   .

The ideal rig would probably consist of a rod similar to that used on inland black bass, saving that it should be fabricated of glass to combat moisture and corrosion. Since resilience is always demanded of a rod to be used on weakfish, a relatively long tip is valuable. Add a well made quadruple multiplying reel filled with a hundred yards of nine to twelve-pound test braided nylon, or nylon monofilament if the reel is designed to handle that material, and the basic outfit is complete.

Once thought to be indispensable on any weakfishing grounds, the famous old popping rod has been largely replaced by spinning and plug casting combinations. This is a logical trend, since the popping rod is no more or less than a connecting link between the bait and surf stick. It's a light, relatively long and resilient rod designed to cast small artificials or a popping cork rigged ahead of live or artificial baits.

The traditional popping rod is nowadays something of a rarity along the North Atlantic coast, but it is popular in Florida and throughout the Gulf of Mexico. Moreover, as will be seen, variations of the rig are employed in surf casting and trolling along the entire seaboard. However, like the big squidding outfit, the true popping combination has come to be a regional weapon.

Modern popping rods should be made of glass (although a great majority are still constructed of split bamboo or natural cane) and measure approximately eight feet from butt to tiptop. A light tip and soft action is to be preferred and the rod should handle lure weights in the one- to two-and-a-half-ounce range. Any good service, bay or small surf reel filled with 15- to 18-pound test nylon braid, or one of the new, medium sized salt water bait casting reels which are designed to take monofilament lines make an excellent choice.

This outfit can be used for surf casting—and *is* used under the nom de plume of a "light squidding rig." Surf casting gear, on weakfish, is almost never employed south of Hatteras and, even in the northern coastal range of the fish, those weakies taken from the outer shores are invariably snagged while anglers are seeking a mixed bag of striped bass, bluefish, kingfish and other inshore gamesters. There are notable exceptions: when weakfish are plentiful, New Jersey beaches often produce exceptionally fine catches on the long rod.

Roughly speaking, there is no specific surf rod type designed for weakfish alone, nor is there any reason to wonder at this state of affairs. All surf rods are designed as "casting" rather than "fighting" instruments. Since weakies taken in the surf are generally within easy casting range and are willing to take such lightweight lures as the various bucktails, tin squids and midget plugs (as well as fresh bait), the heft of the outfit is dictated by the presense of other and larger fish in the area. Invariably, the light squidding outfit—something approaching a beefed-up popping rod— is sufficient. Here you have the first instance of a northern popping rod under another name.

In surf casting for weakfish, where an occasional striped bass or bluefish may stick his pugnacious nose into the party, the eight- to nine-foot light glass surf stick which is designed to cast lures in the one- to two-ounce weight bracket is well chosen. A wide spooled squidding reel filled with a 27-pound test braided nylon, or one of the new monofilament reels loaded with 15-pound test mono completes the rig.

This tendency to use monofilament line has invaded all of the accepted techniques in weakfishing. Mono is the first choice in spinning, indeed the only logical choice when lines test at anything less than ten pounds. It can be put to good use in bait casting, popping, in light squidding and trolling. Even the fly rod enthusiast agrees that mono is without a peer in live-lining bait through a chum streak.

Fly fishing for weakies, it must be admitted, is often a misnomer in the north. Although the species can be taken, and taken in numbers, with small feather artificials and popping bugs, a majority of sportsmen who use the long wand are particularly interested in baiting the fish in a chum streak, or in drifting a bait over a good stretch of water. Artificial flies can pay off when they are drifted into such a chum streak, and it is thus that the greater percentage of weakfish are taken "on a fly" in northern climes. Do not, however, conclude that the light feather or cork-bodied artificial fails to take seatrout; anglers who specialize in this type of angling find the species receptive to a variety of fly rod lures.

The fly rod to be used on salt water should be fabricated of glass, which is impervious to moisture. While split bamboo will do the trick—and pleasantly—the bamboo article, unless specially treated, is always subject to deterioration when it comes in contact with salt water. Therefore, as practical fishermen, we invariably choose glass sticks for use on the sea front.

If the angler plans to cast artificial flies and bugs, the rod he chooses must be capable of shooting line into a considerable breeze. For that reason, and not because its power is needed to fight a big fish, the outfit that has come to be standard on southern bonefish flats and tarpon grounds is equally effective on trout. The rod should measure approximately nine feet from butt to tip, feature a relatively soft action combined with plenty of backbone, and weigh six to seven and one half ounces.

Any of the fine single action reels now on the market will suffice for use on southern spotted or northern weakfish. Line, always a treated nylon or dacron, should balance the rod's action—and note that the heavy outfit usually takes a GBG or, better, a GAF torpedo. Eight or nine feet of tapered monofilament leader completes the outfit.

In live-lining a chum streak, or in drift fishing across a bay, grass flat or inlet, the single action reel filled with eight- to ten-pound test monofilament is a grand choice. While it is impossible to "fly cast" with mono, an angler soon discovers that he can flip a bait for a considerable distance, using the technique which has been called "loose leaf spinning." Simply stated, this entails stripping a half-dozen coils of mono off the single action spool and making the cast as it would ordinarily be made with a spinning reel.

And why not use a spinning reel for this office? It has been done, and successfully, but there is the matter of control over bait action with a hand-retrieve. Once a big fish strikes, the fight should be made from the reel, with the rod tip held high to prevent any sudden flurry or change of direction on the part of the fish from parting terminal gear or pulling the hook free. Obviously, the longer and softer action of the fly rod offers further insurance against breaking off.

Let us, here and now, somewhat depart from our usual conviction that boat fisherman should always use boat rods in trolling. While this is generally true, it does not apply on the seatrout's stamping grounds. Spinning, bait casting and popping outfits are all well suited to light trolling, and the fly rod is often remarkably effective.

These rigs afford remarkable versatility since the angler can switch from trolling to casting without the usual change of basic tackle.

Unless you choose to regard the time-honored cane pole as a prototype, there is no such thing as a trolling outfit designed specifically for weakfishing. A few trollers use light boat rods and bay reels, but the majority favor spinning, fly casting, bait casting or popping outfits for the work. That's because the soft mouth of the weakie indicates the need for an exceptionally resilient tip.

Ideally, an outfit designed for trolling alone consists of a light glass tip measuring six feet, coupled to the usual 18-inch boat fishing butt, a revolving spool reel of the service type filled with 18-pound test braid, or one of the latest designs which take monofilament in 10- to 15-pound test. The latter is, certainly, effective in all-around trolling.

Obviously, we have here described a stubby version of the famous old popping rod. It's another instance of "a rose by any other name" and proof that good tackle combinations seldom disappear but undergo variation to suit local needs.

Excepting the cane pole, which is most often employed in bait fishing, close range popping or slow trolling with a short length of line to which is affixed a bucktail jig, the foregoing tackle combinations are most important in modern weakfishing. Some, like the spinning rigs, are used along the entire Atlantic and Gulf coasts. Others are favored in specific locations—and for good reasons.

Surf fishermen who range the beaches of New York, New Jersey and the New England states have always greeted a run of big yellowfin tiderunners by breaking out light squidding outfits. At the same time, northern anglers prefer fly rods, spinning and bait casting tackle for use on weakies in sheltered bays, or when the species can be fished from small boats.

Progressing southward, you find spinning, bait casting and popping outfits employed from the beaches, from bridges, piers and from anchored or drifting boats. Florida's anglers are convinced that spinning is the way to a seatrout's heart, but the vote is not unanimous. Thousands of veterans continue to use bait casting tackle on the grass flats and inland waterways. There is, in addition, a sizeable contingent of folk who continue to boat good catches of trout with the popping rod, another army that swears by the fly rod—and more thousands who troll or suspend fresh shrimp from the tip of a cane pole.

Fishermen of the Gulf Coast employ bait casting, spinning, popping, fly rod and cane pole gear. From Alabama south and west to Texas and Mexico, popping is an important technique which takes many thousands of pounds of trout during each year. Here, as in Florida, a great deal of night fishing is done by seatrout enthusiasts—and this dark of the moon angling is at its best around the flaming offshore oil structures. Weakies, both the northern and southern variety, are attracted by artificial light, or, more literally, attracted to the bait which swarms in the vicinity of a light.

Regardless of the tackle combination chosen, the angler who seeks this beautiful and generally obliging coastal scrapper should always remember that the success or failure of his fishing trip may depend on a wise choice of terminal tackle and accessories. While baits, lures and hook sizes vary, depending upon the size of weakfish in attendance and the fishing methods employed, certain rules are coastal in application.

It is, for example, considered the better part of valor to employ a short trace of wire when angling for really big tiderunners. Although the weakie has no chopping teeth comparable to those of a bluefish, he boasts a pair of extremely sharp canines in his upper jaw. Short leaders of nylon monofilament testing ten to fifteen pounds are usually safe, and no leader is required in spin-fishing the little fellows.

Hook sizes are almost entirely decided by local option. Generally, when big seatrout are in the offing and are taken on tin squids or bucktails, ordinary O'Shaughnessys in 1/0 to 3/0 are effective. A great many bait fishermen rightly prefer small, fine wire Carlisle, Limerick and Sproat bends, and there is much to be said for a snelled hook which facilitates the hooking of minnows, squid or grass shrimp. Larger southern shrimp are generally hooked through the carapace, or through the horn on the head.

Contrary to popular belief, big hooks are seldom required. At Cocoa, Florida, an area which is dedicated to seatrout fishing (and king-sized seatrout at that) enthusiasts who specialize in live-lining shrimp in a tidal flow favor a single Number six treble hook, one barb of which is thrust through the carapace or through the horn of the bait. Similarly, single and double hooks in sizes 2 to 1/0 have always been popular on the Rhode Island squeteague grounds and on New York's Peconic Bay.

The complete weakfisherman should carry an assortment of hooks, small swivels, split shot and sinkers in his kit. Sinkers should range from the minimum split BB shot, through two and three ounces, for it is often necessary to present bait at a specific level—which may vary from the surface to a foot or so off the bottom. Ordinary bottle corks can be utilized as floats, although a majority of anglers who engage in the art of popping are well equipped with the standard rigs which will be examined in another chapter.

Regardless of whether the seatrout fisherman plies his

happy trade from a boat, from a pier or from a beach, he will need some sort of a container for bait—always assuming that bait will be used. Gulf of Mexico skiffs are often fitted with a bait well, but the wading angler or the pier fisherman needs some suitable container to hold that piece de resistance—the shrimp.

Northern grass shrimp appear to thrive in a mixture of wooden shavings; indeed they're sold that way, packaged in quart boxes made of cardboard. If the shrimp are to be kept for any length of time, however, they should be placed under mild refrigeration. One excellent container, the Bait Canteen, is constructed of porous fiberboard and is compartmented by means of a wire mesh tray. Fill the bottom of the box with cracked ice, cover the wire mesh tray with a square of damp burlap—and the shrimp, flipping about over the burlap surface, will be happy. One word of caution: fresh water quickly kills shrimp.

Large southern prawns should be kept in thoroughly aerated sea water. Bait buckets are the obvious choice, and the bucket should be one with a snap-lock lid so that it can be lowered over the side of a small boat, dericked into the water from a bridge span or floated in the wake of a wading angler.

Sportsmen who wade for weakfish need, in addition to a bait container, some sort of gaff, fish gripper or net, a shoulder bag to hold any number of items, and a stringer. The net, gaff or gripper is particularly important, for one must always bear in mind the fact that a weakfish has a soft mouth. For that reason, never try to "stop" a seatrout during its first, powerful run, or assume that you can increase the pressure on a fish as it tires. To do so often means the loss of the fish.

Obviously, throughout this chapter, we have indicated a definite leaning toward the fiber-glass rod, a product made possible by wartime research in the early forties. This preference is not dictated by the belief that glass is superior in action to split bamboo, but is predicated solely on the basis of practicability.

Fine split bamboo rods take an awful beating on the sea front and therefore require a lot of maintenance. Metal sticks corrode or rust, while natural cane is heavy and subject to breakage. Glass, alone, resists the corrosive, grinding and rotting attacks of salt water and sand.

For the same reason, all guides and fittings on a salt water fishing rod should be fabricated of corrosion resistant metal, so that maintenance will be limited to the cleaning and occasional oiling of ferrules, plus infrequent replacement of windings. There is no criterion among glass rods; all of the nationally advertised products are excellent and sell at a reasonable price. Your only problem lies in choosing a rod that is designed to do the work required.

The same may be said of reels. Any good fresh water spinning, bait casting or single action reel can be put to use in weakfishing—but it is wise to choose those models which are built of corrosion resistant materials. Fortunately for the sportsman, there's a wide selection on the market—many of them designed for light salt water work and priced to please the average citizen. Service, bay and light squidding reels take a great deal of punishment in stride and require little maintenance.

Never stress power in choosing tackle to be used on weakfish. The major requirement in a rod is resilience, while the reel should be reasonably well-constructed and feature a smooth, adjustable drag. Seatrout are not tacklebusters, but they rarely accommodate a heavy-handed angler. Play 'em nice, play 'em careful—and you'll rack up prize catches.

CHAPTER 3

Artificial Lures That Catch Weakfish

A SURFACE-FEEDING WEAKFISH OR SOUTHERN SEATROUT (YOU can group the species in this respect) seldom fails to amaze the average angler. Old Specks rarely comes clear after the manner of a tarpon, nor does he cartwheel on the surface like a striped bass, explode like a hungry snook or, half submerged, shoot off in all directions like a jack crevalle. Instead, the seatrout's swirling break is a promise of things to come; it's a powerful, ponderous and heart-clutching surge that is guaranteed to fever a sportsman's imagination.

To see that characteristic half-submerged boil on the mirrored face of a bay or inlet during the mystic, rainbow-tinted half light of dawn, and to catch a glimpse of a broad, square tail curving back into the dawn colored ripples—that's enough to ruin a man's timing. Under these circumstances, no angler worthy of his salt should ever feel it necessary to alibi a backlash!

47

Some of the most exciting fishing on the Atlantic seaboard is reserved for the lad who uses artificial lures on weakies—and, although it is not generally known, the northern as well as the southern species will, at times, wallop a well-placed plug, spoon, squid, fly or popping bug. The strike is sudden, jolting—and the run that follows does credit to a great sport fish.

Hundreds of modern lures will take weakfish and, although some are more effective than others, the observant angler will discover that it pays to be versatile. A change of pace often brings results when the old favorites are not coaxing strikes. Similarly, a change of speed in the retrieve or a radical departure from the locally accepted method of "fishing" a lure may well mean success. For every choice of artificial, there appears to be three separate methods of employment. Strangely enough, every single one of them is right!

If the average angler could bring together, in one group, a panel of expert weakfishermen from northern and southern hot spots, he'd be properly amazed at the variety of techniques favored along the seaboard. A squeteague fishing enthusiast from Rhode Island's Nayatt Point, in Narragansett Bay, might scoff at the effective use of any artificial other than a gaudy streamer fly jigged in a chum streak of grass shrimp. Spin-casters of New York and New Jersey would certainly point to the bucktail or bullhead lure as a murderous weapon and they would, generally, be seconded by southern sports.

South of New Jersey, however, the trend in artificials begins to include a variety of plugs and combination lures which include a floating splasher to attract the fish and a sub-surface bucktail as the "bait." Add artificial flies and cork-bodied bugs, spinners, spoons and even a strip of white nylon fixed to a short-shanked Number 4 hook, and the possibilities (without going into artificial lure and live bait combinations) appear legion.

Further, just as anglers who fish certain locations along the Atlantic and Gulf coasts prefer specific lures, each section has its own ideas on presentation. The northern fly fisherman jigs his streamer flies in a chum streak while his southern brother casts the feather lure to a feeding trout. Yankee anglers bet on orange and white, green and white and red and white, while John Reb invariably settles for yellow, red and yellow or red and white. Both groups have reached their conclusions through trial and error.

Take, for example, the bucktail fishing technique of a man like Morrie Upperman of Atlantic City, New Jersey. Morrie knows every channel and hole in the Great Egg Harbor section and he takes a lot of weakies on those famous bucktails which he and his brother, Bill, manufacture.

Upperman's technique, and that of a majority of New Jersey anglers, is to cast up and across the current. The retrieve is relatively slow, with the lure bouncing over the bottom, darting in the tideway and simulating a shrimp or a bait fish caught in the inexorable grip of a strong current. Morrie catches fish, but his bucktail technique would be questioned by a Floridian like Ernest Lyons of Stuart.

Ernie is a seatrout angler who knows just about all there is to know about the wonderful specks of his great Indian River—St. Lucie Inlet country. He uses the bucktail lure and he uses plugs—but Upperman's slow, cross-current retrieve is not for Lyons. Floridians prefer to use a method which, for want of a better name, has been called the "Florida Whip."

In this retrieve, the lure is cast across or with the

current and is brought back in a series of sharp hops, accomplished by violently whipping the rod tip. The theory behind this retrieve holds that all lures used on seatrout should simulate a fast moving shrimp—and the method is almost universally employed in Florida. There is only one area of the Sunshine State which disagrees—and in this section plugs are used to the almost complete exclusion of the bucktail.

Ask Gary Bennett of Cocoa, Florida, and he'll tell you that a big trout likes plugs—and that they like plugs retrieved at slow speed. Cocoa regulars score with a variety of wooden lures, but several specific models are the killers. Moreover, Cocoa's top fishermen like to chase seatrout at night, a practice which is uncommon along the North Atlantic coast but which assumes greater importance in Florida and the Gulf of Mexico. Night fishing is particularly profitable around the offshore oil rigs in Louisiana, Alabama and Texas.

Any given method is the result of trial and error in a specific location and is most likely to succeed in the area of its popularity. Nevertheless, a slavish obedience to custom is unwise when the local technique fails to produce. Morrie Upperman's slow, cross-current retrieve is admirably suited to the water he fishes, yet the "Florida Whip" will take trout at Great Egg Harbor Bay. Similarly, you can hook St. Lucie specks on the New Jersey retrieve—and take Cocoa's seatrout with either method. What we're trying to emphasize is the fact that no stereotyped technique is infallible.

Weakfish and seatrout are always likely to grab unusual lures. Back in immediate postwar years we took a number of big weakfish from the Cape Cod Canal in Massachusetts. Practically all of these fish hit huge eelskin rigs intended to lure striped bass. Canal regulars also caught weakies at night, under the artificial lights of the Cape's big ditch, at a time when northern weakfish weren't supposed to be night feeders. Most of these scrappers were lured to single sperling, blueback herring or menhaden fry presented on a single hook.

Artificial flies might have worked as well—and there's little reason to believe that pattern would have been important. Floridians who spend the long night hours catching shrimp with the aid of long-handled nets and gasoline lanterns suspended from bridge railings, also take thousands of small seatrout on a strip of white nylon binding tape, cut to one-inch length and attached to a single, small hook. This curious on-the-spot "fly" is dapped back and forth on the surface—and it appears to be a killer!

The lure that works in one locality may not work in another, but the opposite is often true. For example, reams of type have proclaimed to the world the fact that northern weakfish are scared out of a year's growth by the sound of an oar clunking on a cedar gunwale (true) and that southern spotted weakfish or seatrout are intrigued by the sound of a popping cork (also true) but there has been little correlation of the information. Both northern and southern varieties are extremely sensitive to noise or vibration, both are frightened by *foreign* sounds—and both will come to a surface commotion lure.

A popping bug, for example, will take a northern weakfish—though not as readily as it will lure a southern spotted trout. Such catches, in the north, are usually made during the hours of darkness. The limiting factor may well be water temperature. When the sea is cold, weakies are less active, feed at the bottom or loaf around the mid-depths. A sudden drop in temperature will cause the southern variety to dive into deep water and to copy the early spring performance of its northern cousin. Because southern waters are generally warm, surface feeding tendencies are emphasized.

Practically all of America's artificial lures are effective on weakfish but one type is, on a coastwide basis, most effective. This is the bucktail jig, also called the bullhead, the doodlebug, the bugeye, the barracuda or the feather, depending upon local usage. Employed with or without a pork rind trailer or some "sweetening" agent such as a strip of squid, the bucktail is the most important of all artificials used on this species.

Basically, the lure is effective because it resembles a small bait fish or a shrimp. The positioning of the single hook guards against fouling on bottom—although not against floating weed. Actually, when trolled such a lure will gather unto itself far more weed than other lures because the eye of the lure is to the rear of the leading portion. Bits of grass and other debris tend to slide down the leader and catch firmly, which completely ruins any fish-taking possibilities.

Bucktails can be used at mid-depth by means of a rapid, hopping retrieve, or they can be bounced along the bottom. Horizontally flattened types will ride higher than those which are rounded or keeled, but there is little to advocate one model over another.

Size is probably more important than shape—and weakfish dote on small bucktails. Midgets that are suited to casting with light spinning gear or plug casting tackle are to be preferred. Yellow, red and yellow or red and white are, on a coastal basis, the most productive finishes. Weakies will, however, hit the all-white bucktail or any number of color combinations. A black-headed job with brown tail has gained many followers on the Gulf coast.

The importance of size of the lure may be overlooked in many areas. At Lynnhaven in Virginia, size is considered all important. S. Claude Rogers of Virginia Beach, who has made a name for himself in Chesapeake Bay fishing circles, carries a tackle box that would put a dealer to shame. During his regular seatrout trips to the famous Lynnhaven grounds, he is particularly fussy about lure size. We made the mistake of disregarding his advice on this matter to our cost. After some experimentation on our own, we found his selection of size was exactly right —and by that time our boat neighbors had several good fish aboard while we went fishless.

Obviously bucktails are made of bucktail. However, the many other materials such as crimped nylon, ribbon nylon and other synthetics on the market today are now part and parcel of the general type lure. When using these, remember that they have a different bulk in the water than the bucktail itself. Thus a 2/0 bucktail will be a good deal smaller in appearance than a similar lure of the same size made from ribbon nylon.

From all the above, it can be seen that an assortment of colors is not the only factor to consider when selecting these lures. Have also a wide range of sizes in your kit and you will be able to handle weakfish that may have become extremely selective in their general feeding.

Imaginative anglers learn to use a variety of retrieves in fishing this type lure but, in all cases, the end result is an effort to make a chunk of lead and a spray of deer hair, feathers or nylon look like some live sea creature trying to escape from the jaws of a hungry fish. Logically, a slow retrieve should be favored when water temperatures are cold and seatrout are feeding on the bottom. As the thermometer rises, so may the offering—both with regards to depth and speed.

Bucktails are profitably employed in chum streaks, in trolling or in casting from small boats, shores, bridges and piers. The chumming angler is most successful when he employs either of two methods: a twitching mid-depth retrieve through the come-on slick, or jigging, which is accomplished by permitting the lure to sink and then retrieving it in a series of slow hops. The strike invariably comes at the termination of a hop.

Trollers employ the same general tactics, but without the marked success of the stationary angler who is better able to control the action of his lure. However, a slow drift over known weakfishing grounds, coupled with regular jigging to keep the artificial bounding along, often serves to locate fish. Thereafter, Lady Luck may smile on the man who anchors and casts to his quarry, although there are handicaps to such a method as will be discussed later.

Northern spinning enthusiasts are bait casters who usually observe the following rule of thumb in "fishing" a bucktail: they cast up and across the tidal flow, permit the lure to sink and then retrieve it at slow to medium speed. Tip action is used to impart a hopping, darting motion to the bait. Depth attained will, naturally, depend on the force of the current, the weight of the lure and the speed of retrieve.

Floridians also believe in casting across the sweep of tidal currents but many of their great trout fishing areas are located in bays or on offshore grass flats where the tide is negligible. Moreover, anglers of the Deep South often take their fish in exceptionally shoal water.

The "Florida Whip," in which a bucktail or plug is retrieved in a series of herculean jerks, is a vastly speeded-up version of northern cross-current bottom bouncing. It is effective in the south because warm water fish are active and eager to chase a rapidly moving bait, but it should not be considered infallible. The change of pace remains a prime secret of experienced trout fishermen.

Bucktail jigs are often used in combination with surface commotion plugs or popping corks. The jig, in this case, is usually a midget of its clan and is fished behind a floating splasher which may or may not be armed with hooks. This technique was developed in the Gulf of Mexico and is the purist's answer to the popping cork and live shrimp of the commercial angler.

The popper serves a dual purpose: it keeps the following bucktail lure at a specified depth, usually ranging from twelve to fifteen inches, and provides the sort of commotion that brings seatrout racing to the surface. Since the bucktail must be kept in movement to insure its success, the popper and jig combination is fished in a series of twitches which punctuate a slow retrieve.

There are two schools of thought on the make-up of the popper and bucktail combination. One holds that the commotion lure should not be fitted with a hook—to guard against fouling in the cast. The opposition admits that fouling is a hazard, but points to the fact that large trout will often strike at the popper in preference to the following jig. Strangely enough, few anglers in southern waters have experimented with the bucktail on a dropper *ahead* of the popping lure, a trick that works on weakies as well as it works on small striped bass.

Logically, a rig featuring a dropper and a following splasher is more practical than the opposite arrangement. The popper thus acts as a casting weight as well as a lure in itself, while the jig is less likely to foul during the cast. In practice, the time-honored popping cork and following jig (or shrimp) is a deadly weapon, so we see no immediate danger of it disappearing from the sporting scene!

Among the lures which are used on a more or less coastal basis are those artificials called clothespin plugs. Typified by the Porter Sea Hawk, these are made of lead or a lead alloy and are used almost exactly as the bucktail is used. Clothespin plugs are manufactured in several weight ranges and finishes, are usually fitted with one or two treble hooks—and are exceptionally effective on seatrout. They are most often used south of the Chesapeake Bay and have only recently invaded the north, where they are employed on bluefish and stripers, rather than weakfish.

Similarly, wooden and plastic plugs are seldom employed on northern weakies. From the Chesapeake Bay region, south to the Gulf of Mexico, they are a "must" in every angler's tackle box. A surprising variety of lure types are successfully used but, as is always the case, certain models are favored in specific locations. Surface and sub-surface types are equally important and there is a place for the plug that goes deep.

Just as the weakfisherman of the north and his blood brother of the south disagree on the proper employment of a bucktail, pluggers swear by a variety of fishing techniques. Northern sportsmen shouldn't be allowed an opinion, for most of the weakies they land on plugs are taken while angling for other species. The plug comes into its own (so far as weakfish are concerned) south of the Chesapeake Bay and becomes almost a way of life for anglers in certain sections of Florida.

Roughly speaking, southern seatrout fishermen who employ sub-surface plugs favor the rapid reel-and-whip technique which is supposed to simulate a frantic shrimp. The method is highly successful, yet Cocoa, on the famous Indian River, does not subscribe. Veterans who seek huge seatrout in this area, notably at Canaveral Harbor, in the Indian and Banana rivers and in the Barge Canal, practically dream a lure along. The logic holds that big trout are lethargic and unwilling to chase a fast moving bait.

Surface commotion lures are favored by thousands of southern trout fishermen and, here again, there is a difference of opinion on proper retrieve. With the exception of Cocoa, most of Florida and the Gulf advocates a fairly fast retrieve, with plenty of noise and splash. Cocoa sports declare that really big trout have to be goaded into striking and maintain that patience is the secret. A popper is allowed to lie doggo for as much as two minutes before it is twitched forward in a series of gurgling hops. Thereafter, the lure is again permitted to lie dead in the water. After two or three pops, separated by long, suspense-building pauses, the water is expected to erupt in that *impossible*, surging strike of a big trout.

Any small to medium sized plug designed for fresh water black bass will take seatrout, but there are certain killers which should always be included in a well stocked tackle box. These include the MirrOlure, Creek Chub Darter, Boone Needlefish and Porter Popstop. Other effective lures include spin-sized poppers and sub-surface types, particularly those which are fitted with spinners. Although underwater swimming and wriggling lures have never been popular on the trout fishing grounds, they'll take fish.

In selecting a plug to use on seatrout, remember that color and flash are equally important. The employment of spinners, strips of bright metal in a plastic plug—or the very translucence of plastic—intrigues weakies. There is little doubt that yellow, red and yellow or red and white finishes are favored by a majority of anglers, yet thousands of specks are taken on lures painted to resemble natural baits. Shades of yellow may deserve a coastal vote of confidence because they most nearly approximate the color of a shrimp in the water. Blue and white or green and white plugs, on the other hand, simulate small bait fishes.

If bucktails and plugs are the most important weakfishing lures on the Atlantic Coast, the artificial fly certainly ranks third. From Massachusetts to Florida and the Gulf of Mexico, there are thousands of sportsmen who hold that weakies are at their best on the long wand and that any other method used to take the species borders on the crude.

Without any doubt, the streamer fly is the favored offering. Popping bugs, similar to those used on snook, tarpon and inland black bass are effective but are seldom employed north of the Chesapeake Bay. Angling techniques change as you move southward, but all hands agree that the trout likes a big, long and gaudy streamer pattern.

Fly casting for weakfish is not a popular game in the north, but anglers of New York, New Jersey and the New England states use the feather artificial to a certain extent. There, the preferred technique is a long drift into a chum streak, followed by an erratic, darting retrieve. The regulars at Narragansett Bay, Rhode Island, and Peconic Bay, New York, often sweeten the barb with a single grass shrimp—although this is unnecessary when weaks are boiling in a well-prepared chum line.

From the Chesapeake Bay South to Florida and the Gulf of Mexico, orthodox fly casting replaces jigging in a chum streak. Most of the fishing is done from small boats, anchored or drifting over flats and offshore grass beds. There are, however, hundreds of locations where a fly casting enthusiast can take specks from shore, from bridges and piers, or while wading the flats.

Popping bugs are highly effective: the best are cork or plastic bodied, and hollow-headed so that they'll create plenty of surface commotion. When trout are feeding in shoal water, these bugs—again in yellow, red and yellow or red and white—can be deadly weapons. Fished in a series of short pops they bring specks charging to the surface.

Streamer flies are, however, the fly rodders' stand-by. These are invariably big and bright colored, usually constructed of bucktail or saddle hackle, with or without tinselled bodies. Northern anglers lean toward an intricately constructed fly, although the southern combination of a single hook, chenille body and a swatch of red and white bucktail is probably just as interesting to a hungry fish.

Back in 1948, the last year of a great weakfish run at Narragansett Bay, Rhode Island, hundreds of anglers were using streamers tied on long-shanked single and double hooks. The favored patterns were green and white, orange and white, red and white—and a red squirrel, brown bucktail creation that was supposed to represent a shrimp. Many of these New England feather artificials were built on the complicated lines of a landlocked salmon fly, even to silk floss bodies and tinsel ribbing.

The idea of a double hook—and this is the true double, rather than a tandem arrangement of singles with one barb riding ahead of the other—is alleged to offer better holding properties in the mouth of a big weakie. For another reason, the fact that hefty seatrout often strike at the head of a lure, Florida's Dick Splaine developed the *Squeteaguer,* a white bucktail, dun saddle hackle pattern with hooks at head and tail. The *Squeteaguer* offers the added attraction of a small spinner flashing at the nose of the fly.

Long-shanked 1/0 hooks are large enough to arm any fly intended for use on weakfish. However, in order to get the artificial down into payoff territory when trout are feeding at mid-depths, it is sometimes wise to use heavy wire barbs. Some of the finest southern flies, designed by

Joe Brooks, are tied on husky Z-Nickel singles. A spinner, flickering ahead of a fly, is always an attraction, but adds weight and offers wind resistance in casting.

Weakfish will take a surprising variety of spinner and fly combinations: spoons, wobblers and other metal artificials. It is probably safe to say that both the northern and southern varieties can be coaxed to most of the flashers intended for use on black bass and landlocked salmon. We have proved the point to our own satisfaction by taking Gulf of Mexico specks on such Yankee favorites as Stuart's Goldfish, Mooselook Wobbler, Daredevl and the various pearl wobblers.

High riding spoons, particularly those shaped like bait fish, are effective in slow trolling over the grass flats. The action of the lure, plus its metallic flash, appears to draw strikes from fish that fail to see, or do not choose to see, bucktails. Any of the smaller wobblers can be employed in combination with a surface splashing plug.

King-sized wobblers are, of course, the classic tin squids of the north. These lures are traditionally molded of block tin, or a tin-lead-antimony alloy. While tin has a soft, translucent shine that appeals to predaceous fish, chromed lures often turn the trick as well. A killer on big tiderunners, the basic squid is seldom used south of Hatteras (where spin-sized metal wobblers take over) but they are a "must" along the beaches of New Jersey, New York and the New England states.

There are several reasons for this popularity, most important of which is the fact that surf-feeding weakfish are suckers for tin. The lure serves a multiple purpose because it will also coax strikes from striped bass, channel bass, bluefish and kingfish. Weakies like the smaller sizes, with white, yellow or red and white bucktail dressing. There are occasions when a trailing pork rind seems to enhance the fish taking appeal of the lure.

Weakfish make you know it when they strike an artificial of any kind. The jolt is characteristic and is usually followed by one sizzling dash for freedom. Both the southern and the northern varieties cap this first run with a tremendous boil on the surface, after which succeeding runs are much shorter. Ernie Lyons of Stuart, Florida, sums it up this way: "Any seatrout can be stopped within a limit of one hundred yards. Once he wallows, by the rules of the game—he's yours."

Do not, however, assume that the battle is won at this turning point in the struggle. A big tiderunner may take one hundred yards of line in one sustained dash, tire rapidly and appear to be licked. The great danger at this point is the tendency to hurry the fish along, either by pumping or by tightening the drag on the reel. Old timers agree that these are suicidal tactics, for they often cause the hook to keyhole and pull out.

Boat fishermen should always use a net—which is also a handy gadget in shore fishing or wading the flats. Pick gaffs are effective but they injure those trout you intend to release. Fish grippers that close over a weakie's body, behind the gills, are favored by a great many southern sportsmen.

It is, of course, quite possible to play a seatrout to exhaustion and hand-land him. Charley Urban and Frank Morgan, two expert and highly successful fishermen of Cocoa, Florida, not only land their trout this way—but do the job at night while standing in a tidal current at the edge of a drop-off. This practice is not recommended for beginners!

Landing a big weakfish in the surf presents a new problem. Here, as elsewhere in fishing this speedy yet soft-mouthed gamester, a light drag is of first importance. Never tighten the drag, not even when the fish appears to be whipped. Instead, lead the quarry over the combers and let a wave drop him high and dry. Undue pressure exerted against a weakie when that warrior is holding against a tidal flow, or is moving out with a receding wave, will almost always tear the hooks out of the fish's soft mouth.

You'll lose more fish on artificials than on bait, but the scales are somewhat balanced by the furious continuity of action when weakies are in a hitting mood. Moreover, there's the thrill of a solid strike, sometimes missing in bottom bouncing, and the heart-clutching excitement you experience as a big fish wallows on the surface at the end of its first, driving run.

CHAPTER 4

Natural Baits

ALTHOUGH MANY WEAKFISHERMEN WILL CURL THEIR LIPS when natural bait is mentioned, there is little question that a large proportion of the fish taken along the Atlantic and Gulf coasts fall for some sea creature tastefully decorating a hook rather than for an artificial lure. We are not here to argue the merits of one type of fishing over the other: we simply state the fact.

Choice of natural baits for any and all of the weakfish clan is a wide one. Since seatrout of every kind feed on just about every small marine creature that swims, creeps, burrows or walks, the angler can pick and choose among a vast variety. Sometimes availability of the selected bait tips the scales in its favor, sometimes the feeding habits of the moment in a given school will determine the preference and—sometimes—the whim of the angler is the prime factor.

When choosing a natural bait—always assuming that a choice is available—remember that weakfish are primarily hunters, instead of scavengers; they prefer some mouthful which at least looks and smells moderately alive. Ancient and decaying shrimp, seaworms, crabs or minnows have scant appeal. There is one partial exception to this rule in the case of the sand and silver seatrout. These two species, for reasons best known to their own palates, seem to enjoy nibbling on dead shrimp during the spring of the year. However, even at this time, fresh bait is to be preferred over the decayed article.

Shrimp, which we have extolled throughout this volume as the weakfish attractor supreme, make ideal natural baits whether large or small, dead or alive. Although prices are sometimes high, shrimp may be purchased from bait dealers near most of the popular weakfishing grounds. The ardent seatrout man will collect his own.

Several methods may be used in doing this. In the north, a small, fine-meshed dip net is an excellent weapon for the job of taking grass shrimp—and may be used to collect the larger southern prawns. Although stout cheesecloth will serve for netting, plastic mosquito screen material is far superior. The plastic takes punishment without tearing, does not foul or rot, remains rigid for easy manipulation and, with a modicum of care, lasts for years.

While searching for shrimp to be harvested with a dip net, look around old pilings, in the grassy edges of a tidal stream or inlet, around any underwater obstructions and even close to the hull of a floating boat. Often small grass shrimp are difficult to see, but one pass with the net in a likely looking spot will tell you whether or not they are present. Some anglers even go so far as to bait a given area to attract shrimp. Fish scraps and skeletons, crushed shellfish or crabs—even sliced tomatoes will work. By anchoring such materials in a small wire cage, under water, a lunch counter for shrimp can be maintained.

From North Carolina southwards and around Florida's

Silhouette cut of common weakfish.

First stop on a weakfish or seatrout fishing trip is the bait dealer's establishment.

A familiar sight in the South: shrimp netters spending the night scooping up the big Florida shrimp attracted by gasoline lanterns suspended over the water.

Dawn breaks over Cape Cod Canal in Massachusetts. When weakfish are plentiful anglers take them here—often on foot-long eel rigs intended for striped bass.

Seatrout fishing is popular along the coast of North Carolina. These early spring enthusiasts are bottom fishing the surf between Carolina and Kure beaches. *(Photo by W. M. Shaw)*

A net is important in weakfishing, for these fish have soft mouths. The schoolfish shown here were taken from Peconic Bay, Long Island. *(Photo by Vlad Evanoff)*

Charley Whitney trying to handle a couple of anchored fly rods while weakies are boiling in a chum streak.

A picket line of spin-casters work the Banana River at Cocoa, Florida, in the heart of the famous Indian River seatrout country.

These fish have the makings of a splendid fish-fry.

Bill and Morrie Upperman pose with a catch which includes big
weakfish and a single striped bass. Weakies and bass are often taken
in same general area and on same lures or baits.

Jean Crooks of Miami, Florida, and Joe Brooks of Richmond, Virginia, admire a spotted seatrout that Joe has just landed on a surface commotion plug. Catch was made in the Coot Bay—Shark River country on the southern Gulf Coast of Florida.

Surf casting for weakfish employing light surf outfits are almost entirely a northern game, reaching its peak from Chesapeake Bay to southern New England.

Fishbinder rig, "doodlebug" float and seaworm-squid combination bait used on weakies along the northeast coast.

Small boats anchored in the tideway at LynnHaven, Virginia. Anglers are using bucktails to take southern spotted weakfish.

Charles Anderson of Florida, takes seatrout from a drifting boat at Cocoa, Florida.

Charley Urban, one of Cocoa, Florida's expert seatrout fishermen, uses a spinning outfit with six-pound test line to land "button trout" in the Banana River section.

Trout fishing is a year round proposition in South Carolina, Georgia, Florida and the Gulf States.

This is one way to hook a shrimp—the greatest of all weakfish and seatrout baits in the Deep South—so that it will remain alive and kicking.

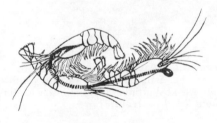

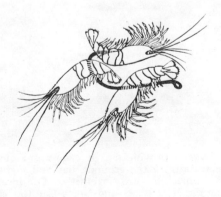

Two methods for threading grass shrimp on a single hook in angling for common weakfish.

Dan Holt uses an ordinary galvanized bucket for a tackle box. He's an advocate of the orthodox plug casting outfit—a rig chosen by thousands of weakfishermen from southern Jersey to northern Florida. *(Photo by Jim Hardie)*

Cape Cod beach buggies provide mobile campsites along the coast, permit anglers to remain on the grounds, day and night, when the fish are hitting. Such machines are currently used to locate surf running weakies along the New Jersey and North Carolina coasts.

Charles Whitney of Shrewsbury, Massachusetts, plays a weakie on a flyrod at Canaveral Harbor, near Cocoa, Florida.

Pier fishermen catch tons of trout along the Atlantic and Gulf coasts. This is a typical trout fishing hot spot, the Williams Steel Fishing Pier at Virginia Beach, Virginia.

Sport fisherman from the Chesapeake Bay on south to the Gulf of Mexico take exceptionally good catches of seatrout from piers. This structure is in South Carolina.

Veterans troll only to locate weakfish. Once located, the most effective fishing method is casting. Shown here, Morrie Upperman and Hal Lyman.

Gayle DeCamp of Orlando, Florida, whips a big seatrout at Canaveral Harbor, Cocoa. Note floating bait bucket which keeps shrimp alive and healthy.

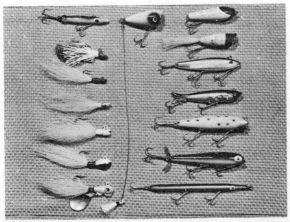

A shoal of popular, artificial weakfish lures. Top left, the SeaHawk or clothespin plug. Right under SeaHawk are bucktails. Plugs (right) include famous killers: from top to bottom, Leaping Lena, Phillips popper, Mirrolure, Pico Mullet, Creek Chub Darter, Porter Popstop and Boone Needlefish. Center, Whopper-Stopper Pop'n'Jig, a modern popping cork with bucktail trailer combination.

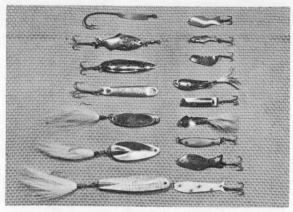

Metal lures employed along the coast. Top left, the ancient pearl wobbler often used with strip of squid or pork ring. From top to bottom, left column: Pflueger Last Word, Acme Fiord, Hopkins No-Eql, Acme Kastmaster, Point Judith Wobbler and Ferron squid. Fresh water lures that take seatrout include, right, from top to bottom: Al's Goldfish, Pflueger Pippin, Pflueger Limper, Roes Crippled Alewife, South Bend Super-Duper, Accetta Pet, Phantom Wobbler, Goldfish and Mooselook Wobbler.

Fly rod artificials that take seatrout include, left to right, top row: the simple bucktail, Woolfie plastic shrimp and breather-type hackle fly. Center, single-hooked streamer pattern and two Narragansett double-hooked streamers. Below, Paul Kukonen's Rhode Island Grass shrimp, a polar bear and nylon streamer and a Phillips popping bug.

Keys to the Gulf of Mexico, large shrimp of all species are taken in great numbers by night-roving bait seekers using long-handled nets and lanterns. A bridge, pier or even a boat will serve as a base of operations. The lighted lantern is lowered to a point about a foot over the water's surface and, as the milling shrimp are attracted to the beam, they are scooped up. Often it is possible to use a drop net—the type usually employed by crab fishermen—under such lights.

When these bait creatures are plentiful, it is even possible to catch them with a minnow trap which has mesh fine enough to prevent the shrimp's escape. This system does not produce well, however, unless the supply in surrounding waters is ample.

Those selling bait commercially often use a small minnow net, which is either anchored on one end or operated by two people. Keep the lead, or bottom, line on such a net close to the ocean floor for best results. By wading inshore, large schools may often be trapped in a single sweep.

Keeping shrimp once they have been caught is a problem of primary interest to the weakfisherman. Remember that shrimp, no matter what species, should not be packed closely together, should be kept cool, out of the direct rays of the sun—and should *never* be moistened with fresh water. If large quantities are to be held over a period of time, they may be penned in a natural or man-made basin where salt or brackish water flows regularly. Stagnant water will result in a high mortality rate.

Fortunately, today, there are many different types of bait containers on the market which are ideal for holding shrimp. These, for the most part, are made of a material which is more or less porous. This insures a good circulation of cool air and, if kept moist with sea water, also means low temperatures caused by evaporation. Additional refrigeration may be obtained by placing a sealed jar of ice cubes in the bait box. Be sure that the seal is tight or fresh water will do its work and the shrimp will die by the dozens. The Bait Canteen, mentioned in Chapter 2, solves this problem by means of a wire tray, beneath which cracked ice provides a healthy living temperature for grass shrimp.

Sawdust, bran or rolled oats are all use as bedding when a container without a mesh tray is used. There is also on the market a manufactured bedding which is almost a powder when dry, yet which looks like a mass of angleworm casts when moist. By removing the dead shrimp whenever found, it is possible to keep bait alive for long periods. Cheaper bedding is adequate when the shrimp are to be used quickly in chumming—and the bedding further serves to "stretch" the chum.

We have gone into considerable detail on the catching and keeping of shrimp simply because angling literature on the topic is extremely scanty and scattered. Since shrimp are the favorites of the weakfisherman, this seems as good a place as any to gather the facts together.

Placing shrimp on the hook may seem a simple task— yet some of those who seek seatrout have developed it to a fine art. There are those who use a fine-wire hook and carefully thread the shrimp over bend and shank. Others use a heavy-wire hook and pierce the carapace of the bait very slightly at the corner so that the critter remains alive and kicking. Some even go so far as to tie the shrimp to the hook with fine thread or with a rubber band. In the Indian River area of Florida, a small treble hook is employed. One barb goes through the carapace or the foremost part of the head, called the horn, and the other two are then ready to catch trout.

We use a combination of all systems from time to time.

With small grass shrimp, we favor threading one or more onto the hook to cover both shank and bend. With larger specimens, such as those found in southern waters, the hook barb thrust through the edge of the carapace or even through the tail section seems to do well. Obviously, the shrimp which have been threaded die almost immediately, yet they still seem to do a good job of catching what they are supposed to catch. If it is possible to keep the bait alive on the hook, by all means do so since it makes the offering more attractive—except for those silver and sand seatrout of the Gulf mentioned a few paragraphs back.

One neglected bait for weakfish—and a bait which looks a good deal like the favored shrimp—is the common sand flea. Although these small creatures are difficult to place on a hook, they do very well for chum when shrimp cannot be obtained. Sand fleas can be found under any pile of seaweed or eelgrass on the beach; they're also attracted to any refuse on the shore and can be caught easily. The simplest system is to pick up the pile of weed and shake it over a piece of spread newspaper.

Because sand fleas are so active, it is difficult to keep them in any standard bait container. By funnelling them into a quart jar from the newspaper, they may be held alive for a short period. However, use them at once for they will die quickly. Such sand flea chum can be used alone in a pinch, but will space out a scanty shrimp supply very nicely.

Found at the shore water-line is another sand dweller which makes an excellent seatrout bait—the sand bug. Although actually a species of small crab, it looks more like an active, sand-colored lump about the size of a dime as it burrows for cover when the water recedes. A few sand bugs can be gathered by digging them out of their burrows, but by far the best way to capture them is to use a "rake" made from plastic mosquito netting. This device, built on the end of a handle, is nothing more than a net box drawn over the sand's surface where bugs have been located.

Here again the bait may be used as chum if a sufficient quantity of sand bugs have been captured. Usually, however, two or more of these diggers are threaded onto a hook. Surf fishermen, simply because of their location when angling, can use them to good advantage—and weakfish gobble the bugs with gusto.

Close cousins to the sand bugs are the crabs—and no matter what crab you mention, a weakfish will eat it if it can be swallowed! Fiddlers, blueclaws, green crabs and all the others make excellent bait, either whole or cut into pieces. Shedder or peeler crabs—those of any species which are just about to cast off their shells—are favorites, as are the softshells, which compose the group that have already lost their shells. The latter are often difficult to find since they hide under rocky cover until Mother Nature once more protects them with a hard coat.

Crabs are where you find them—which is a sweeping statement, but a true one. Fiddlers and sand crabs live in burrows at the tide line. The swimming and walking crabs of other species lurk almost everywhere, but seem to prefer bays and estuaries. To catch them, a crab pot, dip net, or even a chicken head on the end of a piece of string may be used.

Once caught, crabs may be kept hale and hearty in any bait container or box. Put some wet eelgrass or a piece of wet burlap on the bottom of the box and keep them cool. Note, however, that crabs are a quarrelsome group and, if left for any length of time, will kill each other off at a rate of speed which makes the highway traffic casualties look tame. And—*never* keep softshells with hard crabs or, in a matter of minutes you will end up with no softshells!

When using crabs for bait there are various techniques which make them more appealing to a weakfish. Small members of the clan, like fiddlers and sand crabs, should be used whole. One easy way of placing them on a hook is to remove the two hind legs and then run the hook point and bend through the space thus made. The barb should be clear so that it will penetrate a seatrout's mouth when that worthy takes the bait.

Larger crabs should be cut up to make the most tasty lure. Cut them from between the eyes back to the rear of the shell. If they are still too big for the hook, cut again at right angles to this line. It is well to run the hook through some of the firmer tissues so that a slight nibble will not remove the meat from the hook.

Some anglers leave the large claws on the bait chunk. However, the claw meat itself is especially good for taking seatrout. Rather than remove the meat from the claw, smash the claw under your heel or crack it with a knife handle. Incidentally, do not do this smashing on the floorboards or the deck of a boat unless you want to be quietly murdered by the boat owner. Shell particles which cling to the flesh after you run the hook through will protect the bait from scavengers, to a certain extent at least, and seem to give the offering an added attraction.

Small, whole crabs, particularly softshells, may be floated down the current from a boat, bridge or pier with amazingly successful results. No weight whatsoever, other than that of the crab itself, should be used. Run the hook through the back of the shell so that the point comes out on the underside of the crustacean. Lower this bait gently into the water and it will swim about in a natural manner. By live-lining the crab down current, a great deal of water can be covered. Seatrout—and big ones—will smash such a bait when all other tempters are refused.

A bit of crab meat makes an excellent addition to a hook when used in combination with some other natural bait or even with an artificial lure. Such bait cocktails apparently double the appeal of a single bait alone. Thus, a large shrimp tipped with a bit of crab, a crab chunk decorated with a piece of seaworm or any other assortment placed together on the hook does well.

Crab baits take more fish in the autumn than at any other time. Such is not true of the clam. Whether soft clams, hard clams—known as quohaugs to the New Englander—or sea clams are used, the spring of the year and early summer are the times when they are most successful. South of the Virginia Capes, clams are not a common bait, but north of that point they take both common and spotted weaks with regularity.

Such bait should be fished at or near the bottom. Bait the hook with the meat of the shellfish and either drift or still fish with it. The surfman does well with clams in the early season. When surf fishing, a fishfinder rig is to be preferred because weakfish seem to suck in this bait rather than to strike or bite it. This means that the hook should be set gently after the bait has been picked up and the weak starts to move off with it.

It seems hard to believe that the active and comparatively intelligent squid is a close cousin to the humble clam, but it is true—and the squid, usually cut into short strips, makes a fine bait for weakfish of all species.

Trolled, either alone or with a spinner ahead of it, a strip of squid can do great execution. This same rig will take weaks when live-lined from a bridge, pier or anchored boat. When used as a bottom bait, it is well to cut the squid in strips and place a portion on the hook so that it lies flat along the shank. With a fluttering end waving in the tide and with the addition of a cork just above the hook eye, this natural food is made hightly attractive. Often two hooks, joined eye to bend, are used in trolling and bottom fishing so that short strikes will not be missed.

As with any other weakfish bait, the fresher it is, the better it is. To keep squid in such condition, clean them as soon as caught or bought, then place them where it is cold. A warm and ancient squid is a horrid object and has an aroma all of its own. Fresh squid also may be packed in salt after cleaning if they are to be kept for any length of time without refrigeration, but this is definitely a poor second choice when compared with icing. The salted squid turns bright red—but this doesn't seem to repel weakfish.

Used extensively in northern waters are the various seaworms. Finfish of almost any kind will dine with pleasure on these sand and bloodworms—and weakfish are no exceptions. Most anglers purchase their worm supply from a dealer. If you plan to dig your own from the tidal sand or mud flats, be sure that you have checked with local authorities beforehand. There are many laws regarding such digging and the penalties of violating them often are high. In many areas, local permits may be obtained at minimum cost.

As is true with most natural baits, seaworms should be kept cool and moist. Remove any dead worms from the container because one dead squirmer will mean the death of several more in short order. Use salt water only as a moistening agent. In general, the rules applying to the keeping of shrimp apply also to the keeping of seaworms. However, the bedding should be seaweed, rather than bran or sawdust. The man-made bedding previously mentioned will also work.

When putting a seaworm on the hook for weakfish,

make sure that it lies along the shank in the same manner as a strip of squid. Bunched gobs of worms may take trout upon occasion, but the worm with a wiggle will take a great many more, either trolled, drifted or still fished. Here again, the general rules set forth for strips of squid pertain.

If fishing a chum slick of shrimp or ground fish, one of the best natural baits consists of a whole seaworm live-lined into the streak. Any weaks present will grab this larger morsel more readily than they will grab a bait of the chum itself. Next to the oft-mentioned shrimp, sea-worms will take more weakfish through more of the season than any other bait.

Much higher in the line of marine life are the minnows. In this group of seatrout foods, the mummichubs or killi-fish rank high. These small, brackish water feeders are of two main species—the common, which is found along the entire coast of the Atlantic and Gulf, and the striped, which ranges the tidal Atlantic from Massachusetts to Florida. A close cousin of these is the sheepshead minnow, an equally good bait found from Cape Cod to Texas and inhabiting much the same waters as the common killifish.

Any of these minnows may be taken around the mouths of tidal streams by means of a minnow trap, dip net or minnow seine. Although it is best to keep them in an aerated bucket of brackish water during very warm weather, at other times they will live for hours—even days —simply wrapped in a piece of moistened burlap. This hardiness makes them a favorite with the weakfishermen because they serve as a live bait—which is just that, and which can be readily obtained.

Drifted, live-lined or still fished from either shore or boat, the mummichub clan will attract weaks from a long distance. It is best to hook this bait fish either through the lips or gently through the back, just behind the dorsal fin. Do not drive the hook deep: just impale enough flesh to hold the minnow securely. When rigged in this manner, a chub will remain lively for hours—unless a weakfish gobbles it down. Weaks will hit such a live bait hard, no matter whether fished on the bottom or near the surface.

More common than the killi in southern waters is the mullet. Both small and large mullet and the sucker minnow are used extensively as a seatrout bait. With less tenacity of life than the mummichub, they must be handled and kept more carefully in either a live well or bait bucket. Lip hooking is the preferred method of preparing them for a trout's lunch.

Needlefish is another favorite among southern anglers. This small, billed bait may be taken with a dip net, cast net or larger sweep minnow net. It may also be hooked at the scene of fishing by using a strip of any other fish and a tiny treble hook. When used for trout, the only practical way of placing it on a hook is to impale it through the eyes. However, it may also be fished on a treble hook as described for shrimp. Often a small split shot is added to the leader, ahead of the hook, to keep the bait just below the surface.

Cut bait—a piece of flesh cut from any large bait creature —can also be used to entice weakfish of all species. When still fishing, it ranks low on the list of favorites. If used, it should be cut in strip form and rigged in the manner of squid. Addition of the cork float, under such conditions, just ahead of the hook, improves the action. Such a strip makes a good trolling bait and is selected by many when after big tiderunners. One of the most effective of such baits is one taken from the belly of another weakfish.

A specialized use of cut bait is common along certain sections of the Gulf coast. Small bait fish—usually grunt—

are cut diagonally from the back of the head to the anal fin. The resulting tail section is known as a plug-bait or shiner-tail. The hook point is pushed up through the top leading edge of this chunk so that the whole rig rides through the water in much the same manner as a live fish.

Small pieces of mullet are thrown over the side of the boat as chum. In addition, the surface of the water is thrashed at regular intervals with a long bamboo pole. Some anglers use the pole itself as a rod, but this is not recommended for maximum sport. Seatrout come to investigate the disturbance, see and feed on the mullet scraps and then grab the plug-bait with gusto. The whole illusion is that a group of fish have attacked a school of minnows and have then left for other feeding grounds.

Old timers, who use this method, are careful not to overdo the bamboo pole work. A small disturbance at regular intervals is far better than continued splashing. This trick is particularly effective over shallow grass flats. As with other chumming, the ground mullet should be used sparingly.

A natural bait that was used years ago for seatrout is the common eel. Today, for some reason, this wriggling creature rarely meets with the approval of the modern weakfisherman. There is no reason for this, other than the nuisance of rigging small eels when other baits will do the trick. Actually, small eels—either trolled, drifted, cast or live-lined are extremely effective at the mouths of tidal streams and rivers. They should be fished fairly deep and given as much action as possible by twitching the rod tip.

Small eel bobs, such as those used for striped bass fishing, serve well in such angling. A whole eel itself, with no weight added, makes an excellent lure for tiderunners— and an eel tail mounted on a lead head is a casting killer. Similarly, small eelskins will be grabbed by a weakfish and have the advantage of being more readily prepared than the whole eel itself. Huge eelskin rigs, used on the king-sized striped bass of the north, will take weakies but are rarely used by anglers for this purpose.

There is one great advantage to eels and eelskin rigs when seeking weakfish: the bait will stand up for a long time, even though catches are numerous. The soft mouth of the fish does little damage to the tough skin of the eel and therefore it may be used again and again. It is wise to rig such lures with a wire leader because a stray bluefish can make hash of nylon—and eels are great bluefish tempters.

The toughness of an eel brings up the question of toughness of baits in general. A soft bait, such as a piece of crab or a gob of mussel, lasts for one brief bite—and that is all. Sometimes it does not even last for that length of time and "soaks off" before a fish has a chance to sample the flavor. The bait cocktail previously described may help in such cases—with a tough chunk of squid, for example, holding a soft clam to the hook.

However, the use of rigs with two or more hooks on them is one of the best answers for the weakfisherman. Not only do such rigs provide a double chance of taking a fish before re-baiting, they also allow two or more depths to be fished at the same time.

Such multiple rigs are extremely numerous in design and size. Fundamentally, they consist of a sinker, above which is mounted a snelled hook and, above that, another hook. The number of hooks may be increased to suit the whim of the angler, but more than three make an unwieldy rig. Various metal spreader devices may also be used in such fishing.

The simplest baiting for a two-hook rig is, of course, a whole shrimp or other tempter on each hook. For the weakfisherman, this may be improved considerably. For example, a shrimp on the hook nearest bottom and a live killi on the top hook make a particularly effective combination. Weaks apparently are attracted to the moving minnow and, even though they may not take it, they will grab the shrimp. In general, it is better to have the live bait, whether it is a minnow, crab or seaworm, on the upper hook. Its activity gives added attraction to the lure below and tends to keep the lower bait clear of bottom and therefore out of reach of scavengers.

Double or triple rigs can be used in still fishing, drifting, live-lining and surf fishing. In such places as Peconic Bay, the lower hook is often baited for porgies or scup, while the upper one is designed for the attention of weaks. Hook sizes under such circumstances are tailored to the need. Along the Carolina coast, the lower hook may be a 4/0 or 6/0 baited for channel bass, while the higher sea-trout bait will be impaled on a 1/0. If bait is nibbled off the 1/0 size, select something smaller.

In Chesapeake Bay and in parts of Delaware Bay, an interesting device has been added to such bait rigs. Those who use the gimmick swear by it. Known as a "button," it is simply a tiny piece of colored plastic tubing about half an inch long. Line is attached to the sinker, then is doubled and thrust through the "button." The loop of the snelled hook is then secured to the line loop by a simple whole hitch. When the "button" is snugged up to the snell, it holds the hook firmly in place, yet depth can be changed very quickly as desired. Seatrout anglers in the Chesapeake claim that the colored "button" acts as an attractor—and they further claim that green will work better than red on certain days, blue better than yellow on others. We have not found these "buttons" for sale in tackle stores other than those in the Chesapeake area, but they might well be used with success in different sections.

One word of warning when using any double rigs: do not use hooks with exceptionally long snells. A foot in length is ample and, if the two hooks are to be rigged close together, six inches will suffice. If longer snells are chosen, the tangles that will result are horrible to behold. This applies particularly to the surf angler since he must cast the whole works far through the air.

Those who lower any kind of natural bait into the ocean and then sit like a lump on a log will take far fewer weakfish than anglers who keep their bait moving. A gentle raising and lowering of the rod tip—not enough to lift the sinker clear, but enough to tighten and slacken the line—will make the passing fish more interested in what is offered. Use of a small float when drifting or live-lining does the trick automatically because of wave action on the surface.

Double hooks are also favored by those who combine the natural with the artificial. Small plugs ahead of trailing hooks which carry a strip of squid, shrimp or even a piece of fish belly are used by those after speckled trout. This device is simply an adaptation of the popping cork —but the "cork" in this case carries its own hooks. Another trick is to mount the bait strip ahead of the plug, bucktail or what have you. A passing trout sees the plug apparently chasing a fleeing strip and often will hit that strip with a smash. This, of course, is the dropper rig employed on northern stripers and, for many years, a standard teaser on inland trout.

The Gulf Coast angler and, to a lesser extent, the expert weakfishermen of Florida's east coast, make a specialty of the popping cork with a trailing shrimp. This rig, however, is not drifted but is cast to the fish—often to slicks sighted in shallow water. Experienced anglers avoid tangles by a momentary braking of forward motion at the end of the cast, straightening the rig just before it touches down.

Popping rigs are simplicity itself. An ordinary bottle cork, such as that used to stopper a little brown jug, will turn the trick. The cork is fastened to line or leader, about twenty inches above the hook—or less, depending upon the depth to be fished. A split shot may be used to take the bait down. In action, the rig is tossed to the spot where trout are feeding—the cork is popped loudly, and the angler waits for action.

If seatrout are in the vicinity, that gurgling splash usually brings a swift response. The trout investigates the noise, finds a dangling shrimp and immediately assumes that another seatrout has made a futile pass at the offering. Several firms now manufacture popping floats which are used instead of the time-honored cork, but the technique never varies. Popping is an ancient and an honorable method. What's more—it's deadly.

No matter what bait you may use for weakfish, chances are that the hook size recommended in most angling literature will be too large. Some writers suggest hooks as big as 7/0, and advice on the use of 3/0 and 4/0 hooks is all too common. Because seatrout of all species have tender mouths, there seems to be some sort of belief that a big hook will hold more securely. The exact opposite is true. A 1/0 will hook and hold the largest weakfish that swims and is to be preferred over the larger sizes.

Similarly, the size of wire from which the hook is made should be noted. To present natural bait, light wire does the best job. The jaws of the weakie are not the powerful, shell-cracking weapons carried by the channel bass or striper, so there is little danger of straightening the lighter hooks. Moreover, heavy hooks will buttonhole in the jaw of a weakfish all too quickly—which means a lost fish and a disgruntled angler.

Select your bait carefully, take time in putting it on the hook so that it will appear natural to the fish, place it where seatrout are likely to be, give it action with your rod tip—and the rest will be up to the weakfish themselves. They won't disappoint you!

CHAPTER 5

The Methods—
Fundamental Weakfishing

WHEN THE FIRST PRIMITIVE ANGLER LOWERED A CHUNK OF meat, equipped with an equally primitive hook or gorge, into the water, he started something that has kept fishermen and fish busy ever since. And, undoubtedly the methods which have been tried or are being tried to catch weakfish have provided more than their share of the total business. Because the anglers who seek weakfish are so numerous and because they cover a wide range of waters and climates, the results in development of techniques are extraordinary.

The quest for the species is never-ending. From Mexico's border to the waters of Buzzards Bay, someone is always trying to catch a big string of seatrout. However, success comes mainly to those who know the habits of their quarry, know the various methods of angling which may be used and, most important of all, know just where and when to use one method in preference to another.

In recent years, those who fish with rod and reel around Long Island, New York, have taken almost twice as many weaks as have the commercial fishermen. Despite this fact, hundreds of anglers have returned from these same waters without so much as a nibble from a tiderunner. Similarly, the sport catch of spotted seatrout in North Carolina is about the same as the commercial catch, yet here again hundreds come back from fishing trips with little to show in the way of trout for their efforts.

Chances are better than good that the fishless fishermen were trying the wrong methods even when the fish were within striking distance. Lures are important, bait is important, tackle in general is important—yet none of these amounts to a pinch of dulse if the hook never approaches that soft mouth which has given the species one of its names. Methods vary with the conditions of season, water and weather; with the particular species of weakfish sought; with the section of the coast fished and, finally, with the angling skill of the individual concerned. Most of these factors cannot be controlled directly by the fisherman, but he can adapt his technique to the conditions at hand.

Fundamentally, the methods which take weakfish include trolling, in which a lure or bait is drawn through the water from a moving boat; still fishing, in which a natural bait is lowered into the water from a boat, bridge, pier or shore; casting, in which a lure or bait is tossed in the general direction of the fish, and chumming, in which bait is thrown into the water to attract the fish to the angler's hook. Simple? Not quite! Over the years, anglers have combined all of the fundamental methods in a variety of ways and have thrown in a few dozen wrinkles all their own.

First, let us take a look at trolling. For locating schools

of fish in waters strange to the angler, this method is hard
to beat. However, it has serious disadvantages. As the season progresses and as the weaks tend to feed nearer the
surface, the noise of an engine often will cause the schools
to sound or to scatter. Even the spotted variety, which may
be attracted by surface commotion, may seek other feeding grounds if disturbed by the noise of an inboard or outboard propeller. Another disadvantage is the result of the
feeding habits of the fish themselves. Many times they will
chase bait into the shallows where it is impossible or un-
safe to maneuver with any kind of motorized craft. Under
such circumstances, even trolling with a rowboat using an
"ash breeze" as motive power yields few fish because the
hook will constantly foul on bottom.

When after the common species in the early season and
when after its speckled cousin in cool weather, trolling
provides an excellent way by which fish may be pin-
pointed. At such times, the weakfish are apt to be feeding
fairly deep or resting in some tidal hole waiting for something tasty to swim by. By the same token, trolling will
take both the silver and sand seatrout in the heat of
summer because here again the fish are at or near the
ocean floor. At such depths, motor noise makes little
difference.

Before ardent trollers rise in wrath and cite all sorts of
examples which show that vast quantities of weakfish may
be taken trolling at any time and under any conditions, let
us hasten to say that, upon occasion, spectacular catches
have been made using this method. However, it is primarily a means of locating fish. Once they have been located,
other methods which will be described in a moment will
bring far better success to any angler than will unmodified
trolling.

A fairly long line and comparatively slow boat speeds

are best when after weakfish at considerable depth. Forty feet of line from rod tip to leader is about minimum and we have seen the time in deep water that 100 feet was not too much. Some early season New England weakfishermen use oars exclusively once they are in a likely spot. This indicates that a trolling speed of less than two knots can be ample. In general, throttle the engine down about as slowly as it will go so that the lure or bait almost bumps bottom.

One aid to this type of fishing is monofilament line; it is light, yet will knife down through the water and has the added advantage of being almost invisible to the fish. Naturally, if there are other species around, such as bluefish, add a bit of wire leader for insurance against teeth. If you know the location of deep spots—and a glance at a chart will give this information—drop the rod tip just after the boat passes over the hole. This will cause the lure to sink deeper and will often result in a strike. Some go so far as to throw the reel into free-spool momentarily. However, if the strike comes a bit too soon, the backlash which appears like magic has to be seen to be believed.

For this type of trolling the bullhead type artificial is hard to beat because it does not foul readily when it bumps bottom. Spoons can also be surprisingly successful, particularly when the weakfish are of large size. A small rigged eel or eelskin used to be one of the favorite trolling tempters at the turn of the century—and still works. Among natural baits, a whole minnow, a strip of squid or a seaworm head the list for this method of fishing. The taking ability of any of these is improved greatly if a spinner is rigged ahead of the hook.

Most of this deep trolling is done "blind"—that is, with no indication at the surface that fish may lie below. Once a strike is felt, try to fix the exact spot by noting surrounding landmarks. If this is impossible, toss some sort of marker over the side—a crumpled piece of paper or a small, oily rag will do. Then, if you plan to continue trolling, there will be no difficulty in passing over the same grounds. We do not recommend continuation of this method under such circumstances, but more on that in a few paragraphs.

There is no reason for setting the hook hard if a fish hits while you are trolling: as a matter of fact, there is every reason *not* to set the hook hard. George Brown Goode, writing in 1884 in "The Fisheries and Fishery Industries of the United States," expressed the reason in simple terms: "They bite with a snap, rarely condescending to nibble, and in consequence of the extreme tenderness of the mouth, it requires a constant vigilance to fasten them, and great care to haul them successfully out of the water."

We disagree with author Goode on his classification of the strike of the weakfish, which varies considerably with the method used in fishing for it, but heartily agree with his remark concerning mouths, vigilance and care. Leaning heavily back on the rod when the first tap is felt will end with a hook torn loose—and a lost fish. High boat speeds will bring similar unsatisfactory results.

When trolling for common weaks, seek out the channels in a bay and the drop-off along the shoreline. These locations are particularly productive during the flood tide and the fish will be cruising in search of food at such times. As the tide drops, they are apt to settle down in deep holes where they will lie, comparatively inactive, until the tide floods again. Old timers often claim that these deep-lying weaks will never bite. Such is not the case. It simply takes a little more patience to achieve success—and the lure or bait must be very close to the fish's nose to produce a strike.

For the common species, old wrecks or other underwater obstructions, rotting pilings and similar wood that will harbor marine worms are worth an angling visit. Troll around such objects so that the lure or bait swings in near the obstruction while the boat is heading away from it. This means a zigzag course. It also means more fish on the hook.

Spotted seatrout enjoy feeding around such wreckage, but they are not as apt to haunt these waters as are their common cousins. Because the speckled variety prefers more shallow waters for a meal counter, trolling is even more difficult than for the northern fish. However, this method can be used successfully along the edges of deep channels. Luck will be better if these edges are covered with grass or other marine growth. Such underwater hayfields mean shrimp, and shrimp, as we have said before, mean trout nearby—if there are any trout within feeding distance.

If no charts are handy, the presence of a tide rip will often indicate a hole or bar well below the surface. Troll through such rips with the lure catching the edge of the troubled water. To accomplish this, it is often necessary to have the boat itself some distance up-current from the rip edge. Similar rips where fresh water rivers empty into the sea are productive. The rivers themselves, as far as salt water runs into them—and even above this point—provide some of the best seatrout fishing that can be had.

When trolling in such rivers, do not stick directly to the middle of the channel: run a zigzag course whenever this can be done safely. Better action will be given to the lure if the boat is headed against the current rather than with it. Often strikes can be encouraged by jigging the bait, natural or artificial, so that it moves erratically instead of at a steady pace.

As far as the sand and silver seatrout are concerned, trolling may be considered a minor method. Although they are often taken when after other fish near bottom, still fishing, drifting, casting and all of the in-between combinations are preferred by anglers.

From all of the above, it may seem that we suggest trolling as a means of *locating* weakfish. We do. As a means of catching the critters, trolling is low on our list —and this despite the fact that we will never be able to convert thousands of sportsmen who burn gasoline by the gallon, endlessly dragging a hook through the water in the fond belief that they will shortly fill the boat with fish. Fair success may attend their efforts at times, but the success would be far greater if they stopped roaring around in circles and started serious angling. Among other things, trollers often drive the fish away from those who are using more effective methods in the vicinity.

Ways of catching weakfish may be varied to suit the whim and skill of the fisherman concerned once a good spot has been discovered—and that spot should be marked, either mentally or actually, on a chart. This is not only for fishing at the moment, but for fishing in the future. Unlike many marine species, which may shift their feeding grounds each day, weaks of all species tend to return to the same locality day after day or night after night on the same stages of tide.

One of the best examples to illustrate this point is at Lynnhaven in Virginia. There the regulars, casting from small boats, shift their anchorage at every stage of the tide to follow the schools as they work into the bay on the flood and out again on the ebb. This fleet movement is as regular as clockwork—and it brings results. Naturally a

storm or unfavorable wind may change the routine, yet
when normal weather prevails again, the same system starts
once more.

Common weakfish of school size tend to follow this
feeding pattern more closely than do the big tiderunners,
which cruise either singly or in small pods. Even large
spotted seatrout fall into line to a great degree as do their
smaller school brothers. As far as the small sand and silver
varieties are concerned, they stick to the rule without
notable exception since they are primarily school travel-
lers.

Once a weakfish feeding ground has been located, either
by trolling or through past experience, there are several
methods of attack. For those who are not skilled in casting, the simplest process is that of drifting. First it is
necessary to determine which has the most notable effect
on the movement of the boat—wind or current. If the
wind is stronger, proceed upwind to a point at least twenty
yards from the feeding grounds. By the same token, if the
current has most effect, head up-current the same distance.
Then kill the motor and drift down to the fish.

Either natural or artificial baits may be used, or a
combination of the two can work wonders. Let out enough
line to reach bottom; then reel in a foot or two. As the
boat drifts over the spot, jig the rod tip to give maximum
action to the lure. To determine the depth at which the
fish are feeding, as many as three baits or lures may be
attached to the line with spacing of two foot intervals
between them. At the first strike, note which hook has
been hit and thereafter drift the lures at that depth. If
no strikes result, head upwind or up-current once again,
sound bottom once more, then take in at least eight feet
of line and repeat the drift.

When travelling to the starting point of the drift, never

pass directly over the area where the fish are presumed to be lying. Make a wide circle so that the noise or shadow of the boat will not spook the school. This is particularly important in shallow waters.

Many anglers mark their lines when the proper depth has been found. A simple way of doing this is to tie a small piece of thread just above the reel at the desired point. Today there are various trolling lines on the market which are marked at intervals either by change in color of the line itself or by colored strands worked into the braid. For monofilament or wire line—these last, incidentally, are rarely needed for weakfishing—a tiny dab of colored nail polish serves well.

One highly successful device, borrowed from the fresh water angler, to maintain proper depth during a drift, is a bobber or float. This is particularly effective when natural live bait is being used. A minnow or large shrimp impaled on the hook can swim with a minimum of line drag to weight it down, since the float takes up the slack.

It might be well to note at this point that weakfish of all species vary their strike considerably and that this variation as a general rule depends upon the depth at which they take the hook. At or near bottom, the angler will feel a couple of sharp tugs and the hook should be set gently once such tugs are felt. At mid-depths, the fish seem to mouth the lure. Do not strike at once. Allow the trout to have the hook for a slow count of three and then lift the rod tip. When weaks are at or very near the surface, chances are that they will strike with a savage rush. There is no need to set the hook because the fish does the job. However, there *is* need to hold on to tackle. Many a good outfit now rests on the bottom because a careless angler left it unattended with the reel drag set too tight.

Drift fishing is also highly effective for the caster. Here, nearly the same system is used as described above, but instead of allowing the lure to be carried along only by the motion of the boat, added attraction is given to it by working the rod and reeling in line. One great advantage of casting over simple drifting is that the depth at which fish are feeding may be determined almost at once. In addition, a cast may be aimed at a particular spot which has produced a strike.

Spinning and sea-going bait casting tackle are the most effective for this work. As a general rule, best results are obtained by casting upwind or upcurrent—that is, in the direction opposite that of the direction of boat drift. This often means casting right into the eye of the wind, but still it is to be preferred. When boat movement is rapid, the lure may not reach bottom. In such circumstances, cast in the same direction as the craft is moving and speed up the retrieve.

A beginner at this type of fishing will often wonder why an experienced angler gets two strikes to his one. The answer is in the retrieve of the lure—and the lure, incidentally, is usually an artificial one. On the first cast, allow plenty of time for the hook to reach bottom before turning the reel handle. Some fishermen even pay off line to speed the sounding process. Once the bump, which indicates the ocean floor, is felt, twitch the rod tip smartly, give the reel handle a couple of turns, twitch again and reel again. Keep this up until you score a strike or the lure comes clear of the water. If a hit comes near the surface, there is no need to wait, on future casts, for the artificial to touch bottom.

Speed of retrieve may also be varied—another advantage over simple drifting. When seatrout seem to tap the hook without taking it, speed up the reeling rate. In this method of fishing, a strike is apt to come just as the lure is at the end of its upward travel after the rod tip has been given its jigging action. Watch also for strikes right alongside the boat because a fish will often follow for several yards and then decide to grab the artificial as it heads skyward.

Drifting and casting can be used very effectively for locating schools of seatrout of all species, but particularly the spotted variety—since the method may be employed in shallow water without fear of stampeding the fish. Two anglers, each covering a half circle of water surface from one boat, will soon determine whether there are trout in the area. Neither shallows nor deeps should be neglected and, once a fish has been hooked or a strike felt, both fishermen can concentrate on the payoff spot.

Drifting, whether or not combined with casting, is one of the best ways of catching weakfish. However, all too often it is impossible to use this method. A strong wind or a swift current, a number of boats in the immediate vicinity or a threatening shoal are but a few of the factors which may prevent free movement of a boat. In such cases, the obvious compromise involves the anchor: lower it gently over the side, well above the favored spot and allow wind or current to swing the craft near the fish.

If there is little chop on the surface, a bridle which will permit the boat to swing broadside to wind or current means more fishing room and more comfort. A line run from the stern to the anchor rode will do the trick. After this stern line has been made fast, simply slack off a little more on the anchor and let the engineering force triangle take over.

Once in proper anchored position, casts can be made to cover the water where weaks are presumed to lurk. With no boat motion, it is naturally possible to vary speeds of retrieve, depth of the lure, action given to the lure by rod motion and even to change lures themselves many times. In brief, every trick in the book can be examined while within range of the feeding fish.

There are handicaps to such casting, however. If fishing is good and several trout come over the side, chances are that the remainder of the school will either move off or will stop hitting as they see their companions derricked up into the outside world. When this happens, it is wise to stop fishing entirely for at least five minutes. Continued casting with completely different types of lures spooks the feeders more often than not, while giving them a rest for an appreciable time may well see them back on the job of filling their bellies.

Another disadvantage of an anchored boat is that a hooked weak may dash about among its fellows and they in turn will run into, or be run into, by the line. Once a seatrout has felt the touch of a line on its body, it will rarely investigate anything with a hook in it for some time to come—and may even communicate its fear to the whole school. When playing a catch, therefore, try to steer it away from the spot where it struck.

If tired of casting or if not skilled in the art, an anchored boat is the obvious platform from which to try one of the oldest methods of angling—still fishing. Of course natural bait is to be preferred over artificial lures under such circumstances. Tricks employed when fishing for weaks are numerous and every old timer has a few up his angling sleeve.

Fundamentally, all required are: a hook, a line, a sinker and a piece of bait. Actually, the arrangement of these ingredients can be worked into an amazing number of different combinations, as explained in Chapter 4. When still fishing, lower the sinker to the bottom—and a rounded sinker is best—and then raise it half a foot or a foot. This will allow the bait to drift in a natural manner. If the current is strong, keep the sinker on the bottom and let the hook snell or leader do the drifting.

Sitting thus with a wriggling shrimp, live minnow or crab on the hook may get results. However, a rhythmic raising and lowering of the rod tip will get better. Do not jig the bait as an artificial lure is jigged when drifting: simply lift it gently up and down to obtain enticing action. As in other types of weakfishing, the hook should be set when a fish takes it near bottom just as the slack in the line is straightening out.

Almost always, there will be some current moving by an anchored boat, so "stillfishing" refers to the craft itself, rather than to the hook and line. By taking advantage of such current, the good weakfisherman can make an unskilled companion appear very unskilled indeed. Good results depend upon two major factors: first, presenting the bait at the proper depth; second, giving that bait natural action. As when drifting, the use of two or more hooks hastens the discovery of the proper length of line to use for best effect. Starting with a sinker heavy enough to hold bottom, the weight may be decreased as the bait is brought nearer and nearer the surface.

If seatrout are right on the surface, a single split shot may suffice. No weight at all is needed at times when the current is strong enough to carry the line away from the boat's side and, no matter at what depth the hook rides, it should be remembered that the lighter the sinker, the better the action of the bait. Therefore, use the lightest possible weight the current will permit.

Additional action can be given to the shrimp, minnow, crab or other tidbit not only by manipulation of the rod itself, but also by letting out line and drawing it back again. When this is done with no sinker, or even with a very light one, it is known as live-lining. Live-lining is highly successful in taking weakfish of all species, whether from a boat or from some structure built over the water. Often light artificials are used in this manner with telling effect.

When current is slack and natural bait is the lure, again a float is useful in keeping the hook at the proper depth and also in keeping it away from the side of the boat. Here the difference between fishing for common and spotted weaks becomes very obvious. For the common variety, a quill float is ideal since it presents minimum resistance to the water and allows full manipulation of line and hook. For the speckled, such resistance is welcomed since it acts as an attractor. Big, hollow-headed corks are a familiar sight to the southern angler. "Popped" on the surface, they bring trout swimming to see what is causing all the fuss. This rig also works on the silver and sand varieties.

Perhaps the best known method of fishing for common weaks from a boat—and it can be used in bridge or pier fishing as well—is chumming. (Chumming is highly successful in taking other members of the clan, but has not reached the fine science in southern waters that it has in such locations as New York's Peconic Bay area and Rhode Island's Narragansett Bay.) Briefly, chumming consists of tossing shrimp, cut-up fish, mashed crabs or any other tasty morsels over the side so that a slick is made down-current to form a free lunch path which terminates at the angler's hook.

Of all the attractions used as chum, live shrimp lead the list. Some "stretch" shrimp by mixing uncooked rolled oats, fine wood shavings or other light colored particles with the edible articles. However, the great secret of a good chum streak is steady chumming with a very few shrimp tossed over at a time. Great handfuls thrown into the water at long intervals means great waste.

When the current is strong, a good trick is to pinch the shrimp slightly so that they will not be so active and therefore will not leave the vicinity of the boat so quickly. Another stunt is to toss the chum over the upcurrent side of the craft so that the feed is not washed away so rapidly. Some anglers plunge their hand, holding several shrimp, a foot or so under water and then release the bait. This keeps the shrimp at a good depth and prevents heavy inroads by marauding gulls.

Too much rolled oats or other floating chum "stretcher" will attract gulls in numbers. It is wise to use such materials fairly sparingly. If ground-up fish is being used, plain beach sand will cause it to sink rapidly close to the angler—a handy thing to know when the current is particularly swift. Just mix the chum and sand together in a bucket about one-quarter full of water. The resulting paste may not be attractive to humans, but it definitely is to weakfish. Do not try to use this method with shrimp because the critters will float free of the sand—and often will be killed in the mixing.

When chumming, try to anchor the boat so that the chum streak runs from shallow water into deep. This will draw weaks in a natural path as they seek food—and eventually find a hook. In many cases, use of a natural bait different than that which is being used for chum brings best results. Thus a live minnow, chunk of shedder crab or seaworm live-lined into a chum of shrimp often proves a morsel that is too good for the fish to resist. Similarly, artificial lures, either cast or live-lined and jigged, can take a high toll.

Naturally, the more boats that gather in one area regularly to chum, the better the fishing will be. After a very short time, weakfish will find the free lunch counter always handy and they will therefore swim in that direction in their daily lookout for food. And woe betide the marine hot-rod owner who zips through a well prepared chum slick! A jury of weakfishermen would consider drowning far too gentle a punishment!

Since chum brings the fish near the surface, light tackle may be used to best advantage in a slick. Artificials that work at or near the surface, hooks baited with anything desired and little or no weight added, not only provide maximum sport with the weaks hooked, but also hook more weaks. Here, again, as in drift fishing, it is wise to experiment to discover the proper level for lures. Often additional chumming will cause the level to change, so, if strikes suddenly cease, try varying the depth of the hook.

Keep an eye open down current from the boat. Many times the fish can be seen breaking the surface long before they come within hooking range. Under such circumstances, a well placed cast not only will have a good chance of catching fish but also, even when the lure is not taken, may cause individuals to follow. These adventurers often lead their companions into dangerous waters and the angler profits.

Bridge and pier fishermen miss a good bet when they neglect the attracting powers of a chum streak. All too often, seatrout may be seen feeding or playing on the surface just out of casting range. By dropping a few shrimp into the current every minute or two, such fish may be persuaded to travel along the lunch line until they are within range of a hook.

Incidentally, those who try for weakfish from structures built over the water—and there are thousands of them who do so—have a specialized problem on their hands. A good landing net is an excellent investment when boat fishing; when pier or bridge fishing, it is almost a necessity for bringing big weakies that last few yards to safety. Such a net, with an extra long handle, is standard equipment.

Although it might be considered chumming in the strict sense of the word, southern anglers have developed a method of attracting their quarry to the area they want to fish. This method depends upon the underwater noise made by a pigfish in distress, and was first related to us by Ernie Lyons of Stuart, Florida. It sounds silly, but it works!

First, a medium-sized pigfish is caught on a small bait —which may even be a tiny member of the pigfish's own family. The initial catch will serve as a decoy, so it is attached to a short length of line and lowered into the water beside the angler's boat. Snubbed up and thwarted in its desire to reach bottom, the pigfish emits noises that can be heard by seatrout a considerable distance away. When the trout comes to investigate they find smaller pigfish (tasty morsels from a speck's point of view) swimming cheek by jowl with the larger and more vocal decoy. The fish never realizes that the smaller pigfish are fitted with exceedingly sharps hooks!

This system is used for the most part by boat fishermen —and boat fishermen who are angling commercially—but it can be highly successful for the bridge and pier clans. One shrewd pier operator we know not only chums around his place of business during the seatrout season, but also keeps several pigfish tethered to the pier pilings as an added attraction.

In some cases, anglers using the pigfish-decoy method go so far as to trim the dorsal fin of the unlucky pigfish with scissors or a knife. After this rather cruel treatment, the wounded bait is lowered into the water, where it is

Frank Woolner studies a spotted seatrout he has just taken at the
North Fork of the St. Lucie River, Stuart, Florida.

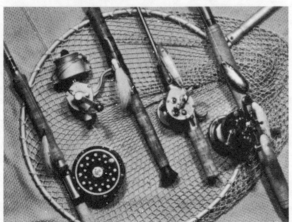

Basic sporting tackle used on all of the weakfish tribe includes the
fly rod, spinning, bait casting and surf rigs, each with typical lure.
Not shown, Texas Popping rod, a light and whippy bait casting-surf
casting hybrid.

A seatrout fisherman relaxes and waits for a strike at Panama City Beach, Panama City, Florida, on the northwest Gulf Coast.

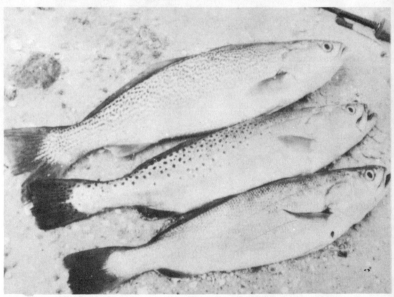

Contrast is shown here among three species of weakfish. From top to bottom—common, spotted and sand.

Typical weakfish of the Narragansett, Rhode Island runs of the late forties. Anglers are Wes Dryden and Dominic Schiavone of Massachusetts who use flies and grass shrimp in a shrimp chum streak to catch fish.

Silvery and small, the sand weakfish is one of the kissin' cousins of the big common and spotted varieties.

Gary Bennett, Mayor of Cocoa, Florida, and an expert angler, takes a string of beautiful seatrout from the Banana River. Cocoa, thanks to Gary—and an abundance of big weakfish—calls itself the "Seatrout Capital of the World."

An angler brings a fish to boat at Peconic Bay, New York, famous northern weakfishing location where fly rods and spinning outfits are generally used.

Joe Brooks, one of America's famous anglers, casts a light bucktail
to a fallen tree in the Everglades section of Florida.

Hal Lyman and Morrie Upperman admire a northern, or common,
weakfish taken on spinning tackle at Great Egg Harbor Bay, near
Atlantic City, New Jersey.

Live-lined shrimp provided this big catch of large to medium-sized spotted seatrout at Canaveral Harbor, near Cocoa, Florida. The angler, Cleve DeCamp uses usual accessories: fish gripper, floating bait car, fish stringer and ditty bag.

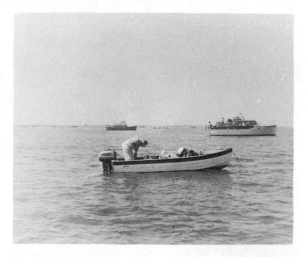

All sorts of water craft, from outboard skiffs to cruisers, gather when Peconic Bay weakfish are in a hitting mood. *(Photo by Vlad Evanoff)*

The tiny, transparent grass shrimp—the principal bait of New England and Connecticut—are always packed in wood shavings.

Mummichogs, called "killifish" in New York and New Jersey, are excellent baits for weakfish and for a number of other sport and game fish along the coast.

Joe Brooks (on these two pages), America's foremost salt-water fly fisherman, whips a long line over a grass bed on the Gulf Coast of Florida. Joe uses a plastic impregnated split bamboo fly rod made by Orvis, a GAF torpedo-head fly line and leaders tapered to six-pound test.

This group of anglers expects action on a rising tide in the marshy salt creeks of the Great Egg Harbor Bay region near Atlantic City, New Jersey.

School weakfish of the north usually average one to two pounds in weight and with the occasional four to five pounders are ideal on a fly rod.

Dan Holt, Carolina Beach, North Carolina, with his 16-foot outboard powered boat. Holt is one of the Tarheel State's greatest sea trout fishermen. *(Photo by Jim Hardie)*

Holt catches a spotted seatrout in the surf at Carolina Beach. The fish fell for a sub-surface plug. *(Photo by Dave Peterson)*

Seatrout often congregate around shell bars, such as this one in Florida's Cape Sable region. The anglers are Ed Louys and Joe Reeves.

Ed Louys and Joe Reeves of Miami outboard across a shallow bay near Cape Sable, Florida, an exceptionally good seatrout fishing water.

The time-honored cane pole is still used on southern weakfish and seatrout. These Miami anglers use the shrimp-and-popping cork method.

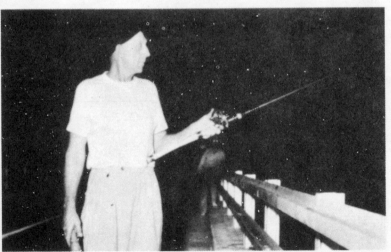

An angler walks along the railing of a Florida Keys bridge, dragging a lure in the water beneath him. Trolling without a boat takes seatrout, snook, tarpon and other game fish. *(Photo by Jim Guy)*

These anglers are seeking seatrout—immensely popular along the Gulf Coast—close to Slidell Bridge over Lake Pontchartrain, Louisiana.

Famous Gandy Bridge, connecting Tampa with St. Petersburg, where anglers fish seatrout and northern weakfish from a special walkway built out over the water.

Anglers cast from a rock jetty at Jacksonville, Florida. Seatrout are popular in this region and individual fish are large in size.

Celia Chaplin of Marathon, Florida, one of the state's expert lady anglers, exhibits a plastic shrimp cage which keeps bait alive while a fisherman wades the flats.

A great deal of night fishing is done in the Cocoa area by seatrout fishermen using waders to protect them from the chilly waters during the fall and winter months.

Bill Curtis, Miami, Florida, uses a footed pole to propel his boat over the flats. This technique is usually employed in bonefishing, but can be equally effective in weakfishing.

expected to make a great and continuous outcry, thus drawing seatrout for leagues around.

All methods of fishing practised from a boat may, with certain obvious modifications, be used from bridges and piers. Trolling, as such, is out of the question: yet, when the area is not crowded, a live bait or artificial may be "walked" along the structure. To do this, the angler simply strolls with the rod over the rail and sufficient line out to reach well below the surface of the water.

In southern waters, the popping cork is a favorite of bridge fishermen. To increase chances of a catch, two rods may be used. The first is braced against the rail and natural bait is the lure. A float is a good idea under such conditions because it keeps the bait clear of pilings and neighboring lines. The second rod is manipulated by the fisherman himself and may present any combination of baits, natural or artificial.

When hooked by a bridge angler, a seatrout often tries to tangle the line in the nearest available piling, rock or abutment. Again, a float is good insurance against such fish tactics. Use of a tight drag on the reel is a poor idea when the trout makes this first dash for it will almost invariably result in a pulled hook. Often there is only one solution—free line combined with a modicum of angling prayers!

Many weakfishermen stop their efforts when the sun drops below the horizon, but there is an army of those who prefer the hours of darkness. In general, all members of the weakfish family tend to come near the surface just as the sun starts to set. Often they will feed voraciously from this moment until the last glow of twilight dies. When darkness falls the fish are apt to sound and thereafter feed deep. Similarly, schools will surface at the first hint of light in the east, feed until sun-up and then either scatter or move toward deeper water. This last pattern of behavior is followed by and large during hot weather.

There are many exceptions to this general rule. Perhaps the most common is that found in Gulf waters. Here, night fishing around oil rigs which burn off waste material through the night, provides excellent sport. Similarly, any fixed light, such as those on offshore oil structures, on bridges, in navigational canals or on any man-made structures, seem to attract bait fish. Seatrout gather to feed on bait and anglers, in turn, are attracted by trout!

In the range of the spotted trout, big fish often move on to the grass flats after dark. They do so particularly on the incoming tide following an extremely warm day, and then the night angler comes into his own.

When fishing after dark, all methods known to daylight angling may be employed. Generally, however, the night operator uses deep running artificials or natural bait presented at or near the bottom. If surface lures are employed, they should be fished very slowly. Natural bait is preferred by most during darkness, not only because of the ease in fishing such a lure, but because smell or taste will attract the quarry more readily.

During darkness, the use of noise as an attractor for spotted seatrout is not as successful as it is when the sun is high. However, it will work on occasion and should be tried when other methods fail. Some southern cane pole fishermen even go so far as to beat the water with the pole tips. Others employ the popping cork previously mentioned. Oddly enough, this disturbance on the surface —which will generally scare common weaks in the daytime —often gets results on the species after dark.

Since surf fishermen are a rugged breed, often they will be found fishing the clock around. Their quarry may not necessarily be weakfish, or weakfish alone, for bluefish, striped bass and channel bass frequent the same waters in many cases. However, the weakfish ranks high among the favorites and attains ever higher rating as the angler moves southward.

This method of fishing is divided into two categories: fishing with natural bait and fishing with artificials. Like so many divisions of the sport, the two overlap so that an angler may use a strip of squid to decorate a regular tinclad jig, or may add a buoyant "doodle-bug" to his hook to make a natural bait more lively.

When rigging for natural bait it is wise to have at least two hooks on the line or leader. The first of these will rest on or near the bottom, while the second will float higher in the water. This floating action may be obtained simply by adding a small cork to the leader just ahead of the hook or by employing a New Jersey doodle-bug, which is a simple lure consisting of a hook decorated with feathers and with a piece of light wood or cork painted to suit the angler's whim. Bait on such a floating lure rides high, keeps clear of many scavengers like crabs and skates, gives added action to the bait and, incidentally, catches more fish.

As in other methods of weakfishing, nylon leaders or snelled hooks are to be preferred over wire—although a short wire trace may be employed on big weaks. Cable-cored nylon is a good material to use if bluefish or other toothed fish are in the vicinity. Dull-finish wire runs third as a choice.

Rarely will a weakfish of any species take a surf caster's bait with a rush. A gentle nibble or mouthing of the bait will be followed by a sharp tug. When the tug is felt, the hook should be set, not hard, but firmly.

Artificial lures, fished alone, on the contrary will often be taken with that dash which characterizes the strike of a weakfish feeding near the surface. Tinclads, bucktails of all types and small plugs are favored. A squid strip or pork rind decorating the first two named often give added fish appeal.

When surf casting, seek out the sloughs and gentle rips. If weaks are sighted breaking the surface—they often will chase bait right into the roll of the breakers—choose an artificial lure over bait every time. Cast ahead or to one side of the school if possible, for the splash of a landing lure may startle the feeders. More often, the line itself, drawn through the center of a school, will spook it.

Usually long casts are not needed to get results. In particular, when natural baits are used, fish may hit almost in the wash. Small weaks, and even tiderunners at times, hug the shore in search of sand fleas and other appetizers brought out from hiding by the wave action. To be ready for either sized fish, it pays to have two sizes of hooks baited, say a 1/0 and a 2. Most of the time, but not, alas, all of the time, the larger fish will choose the larger bait.

Once a weak has been hooked in the surf, never horse it ashore. If you try, chances are that the fish will tear loose and swim on its way. The last few feet of the fight are probably most important. Here, a tight drag on the reel or a little too much enthusiasm will mean a freed catch, or what might have been a catch.

As in other methods of weakfishing, chumming often will help. From the beach, such chumming is not easy, but a floating chum pot filled with ground menhaden or other oily fish works well when the current is setting offshore or along the shore. Anchor the pot and fish your bait or artificial as near the head of the slick as you can—without fouling the anchor line.

A specialized type of chumming will work wonders for a specialized type of shore fishing. In this fishing, the angler wades the grass flats and tosses a shrimp or two into the water as he works along. Sometimes the chum drifts ahead of him, but more often it will drift behind him because best results are obtained by wading up-wind or up-current. Then, a cast or two to the rear may pay off from time to time.

This wading and casting routine is a favorite with the spotted seatrout anglers of the south. Cautious stalking of a grass flat, particularly during dawn and dusk hours, can provide excellent sport. Even after dark, the method produces, but it should be noted that the usual deep running lures for night fishing must here be replaced by surface or slightly sub-surface artificials.

Sea-going bait casting rods, spinning and fly casting outfits are the rule. The reason for this is plain. A heavy lure landing with a mighty splash in shallow water will scare, rather than attract, fish. Lighter lures, tossed with lighter lines and lighter terminal tackle, turns the trick nicely.

In such fishing, do not cast only ahead. Cover as much water as possible on all sides and even in back of you. Trout often will work right up to an angler's feet following the mud stirred up by his walking. As in boat fishing, the strike may come just as the hook is being lifted from the water. So be ready for action right up to that last twist of the reel handle.

Often, when stalking fish in this manner, minnows or other bait may be seen showering from the water ahead of a feeding trout. All other factors being equal, such hungry specimens will be working over the flats, up-wind. Therefore, make the cast land up-wind of the commotion and chances are better than even that your lure will pass ahead of the quarry.

Unfortunately, seatrout do not advertise their presence

by driving bait into the air every time they take a mouthful. However, there often is a distinct slick on the water's surface when they are feeding. (Some old timers maintain that they can smell concentrations of spotted trout, and declare that the scent is similar to that of a slightly spoiled citrus fruit.)

Experienced waders keep moving and casting at a steady rate, always with an eye peeled for weakfish sign. When seen, the cast should be made to the slick edge for best results. Sometimes several fish may be taken from one slick if this practice is followed, while a cast into the center of the spot may yield only one.

Night fishermen who use the wade-and-cast routine are, for the most part, fishing "blind." For this reason, knowledge of the area and the exact structure of the bottom is a necessity to make the most of time and effort. Otherwise, unproductive casting over water which holds little or nothing will be the result. It is wise to study the grounds by daylight, preferably at low tide, before setting out on a nocturnal jaunt. And, remember that a slow retrieve on an artificial lure is the general rule for such dark of the moon angling.

It is not always true that murky waters ruin good weakfishing. Watching grass shrimp dribble through his fingers, the angler anchored off Brandywine Shoal may peer through clouded depths and wonder whether his chum slick is taking effect. More than a thousand miles away, a similar angler squints over the railing of the Gordon Pearson Bridge to Dauphin Island and wonders whether that glimmer far below was a seatrout or an odd light reflection.

The Delaware angler and his Alabama counterpart are experiencing the same trouble from the same cause: the waters in which they are fishing cannot be called crystal clear. The story is the same everywhere for those who seek the weakfish family.

Actually, whether the scene is on Lake Ponchartrain in Louisiana or on Rhode Island's Narragansett Bay, weakfish of all species seem to revel in cloudy waters. Their gills can handle an incredible quantity of silt and mud without damage. Waters that would make a bluefish roll belly up are fine feeding grounds for seatrout.

Dan Holt of Carolina Beach, North Carolina, spends every spare moment in quest of trout. He is a living legend in the area he fishes, and tales of his prowess with a bait casting rod and a small mirror plug are legion. Dan prefers the outgoing tide for his coastal sport, not only because bait of all sorts flows out of the brackish bays nearby, but also because the water is roiled.

"A lot of people make a mistake," Holt told us. "When they see muddy water flowing through clear, they fish the clear. That's because, if they were fish, they'd like the clear water. Seatrout aren't people!"

Dan's remarks hold true along the entire Atlantic and Gulf coasts. Do not throw in the towel just because the waters are murky. Visit the weakfishing grounds, cast artificial lures or the locally favored bait—and you may be pleasantly surprised.

Whether you whip the waters to a froth with the tip of a cane pole, or drop a streamer fly into a chum slick, there is one thing about weakfishing that should never be forgotton—a variation in method may improve results. Such methods and combinations of methods are constantly being revised and improved. Do not be afraid to experiment; you may come up with a fishing modification that will fill the boat.

CHAPTER 6

Boats Away

FROM THE BIG CHARTER BOATS OF PECONIC BAY TO THE SMALL
skiffs of the Florida grass flats, every sort of craft imaginable has been, is being and undoubtedly will be used for
taking weakfish along the coast. There are boats designed
especially for those who seek the striped bass and they are
called, logically enough, bass boats. Similarly, there are
boats used in the pursuit of giant tuna and they in turn
—as might be suspected—are classed as tuna boats. So far
as we know, there is just one type of craft designed primarily for the weakfisherman and it goes by no generic
term.

This craft may be found in Florida, specifically in the
area in and around Cocoa but also at various points along
the southern Atlantic and Gulf coasts. No one design
is exactly like another, but general characteristics are the
same.

Fundamentally, these boats are outboard powered and
measure 14 to 18 feet overall; they feature a flat or modified V-bottom which draws only a few inches of water, and

104

a transom that is either square or slightly sheer. Mounting a motor of 10 horsepower or more, these boats can travel at high speed, yet they can skim over flats that would ground smaller, deeper craft.

Hull design is not the one item that sets these models apart from others, although shallow draft is important enough to be emphasized. Like bonefishing skiffs of similar lines, the ideal weakfishing hull permits high speed in racing from one spot to another, plus the ability to stalk wary game fish over water so thin that a northern angler might think it a heavy dew!

Flats fishing experts of the Deep South take shallow draft for granted. Those who seek seatrout also insist on a wide thwart amidship. Used as a seat or as a casting platform under normal operating conditions, this thwart also serves as the cover of a built-in live bait well.

Sportsmen who plan to concentrate their angling efforts on seatrout in canals, shallows and bays which cannot be reached or adequately covered by wading, can do no better than to select such a vessel. The key characteristics: shallow draft, a minimum of freeboard to defeat wind, and a live bait well to hold shrimp, plus the day's catch.

One thing should be kept in mind if you wish to install a well in a standard skiff's hull. The inlet holes for water should be drilled almost exactly on the waterline as determined when the boat is stationary. If holes are drilled below this point, the well may be sucked dry when you are under way at high speeds. Even if this does not happen, the turbulence caused by forced water transfer from holes in the bottom may be violent enough to kill bait.

In addition to the live well, seatrout skiffs are often fitted with wide thwarts both fore and aft. These serve not only as casting platforms but also as points of observation from which the boat may be poled over the grass flats. By standing on such a thwart, the fisherman obtains an excellent view and can handle both pole and skiff more easily. Equipped with Polaroid glasses, the pole-man can often spot feeding fish under the surface that would be missed by the angler raised to no such vantage point. The thwart, plus the angler's height, adds up to a human flying bridge.

No matter what the design of the boat, some motive power has to be added if anglers are to travel from the dock to the fishing grounds. Outboard motors are, of course, the major propelling devices used on modern small boats, and a mechanically sound motor is an obvious necessity. Unless the fishing trip requires a long run at high speeds, the smaller kickers are entirely satisfactory.

Once on the fishing grounds, unless a slow drift over promising grounds is decided upon, oars should be used to move from one spot to another, or to propel the boat in slow trolling. For shallow water weakfishing, the time-honored Florida bonefish pole is far better than the northern ash breeze. Any angler who combines hunting for the fish with actual fishing will always choose the pole.

This footed staff, so familiar to Florida Keys bonefishermen and seatrout anglers, deserves wider recognition on the salt water front. The pole is a simple ten- to twelve-foot staff, to one end of which are bolted two small, triangular pieces of hardwood. Viewed from the business end, the "foot" has the general outline of a tiny, retreating jet plane. The "wings" give more bearing surface on muddy or marly bottom than would a simple pole, yet there is little water resistance.

For those who use their small craft for many purposes or who rent skiffs from the nearest livery, almost any boat will serve in weakfishing. Obviously, safety should be the first factor to consider. Carry a life preserver cushion or jacket for each passenger aboard, running lights if you will be on the waters during the hours of darkness, a suitable anchor, plus sufficient anchor line, and a fire extinguisher to use in case of an accidental blaze.

Good boating practices are always important; doubly so when anglers are fishing the sea. Moreover, there's a bonus involved. Take the inevitable case of four people crowding into a 12-footer. This makes angling almost impossible and, at the same time, causes a shudder to run through the breasts of all insurance executives. After all, the fisherman is supposed to eat the fish, not vice versa.

Actually, two skiffs carrying two anglers apiece will make a far more efficient team than one skiff alone, no matter how many it may carry. If trolling, the two can troll on parallel courses five or ten yards apart and thus cover a wider stretch of water. If drifting, the same distance between boats will locate fish more readily. While still fishing or poling over flats, two different areas may be selected and a simple system of hand signals arranged to bring the less successful group to the more successful once fish have been located.

When chumming, the bridled boat is the best bet—providing that weather permits this maneuver. If two boats are fishing in company, the system can be carried a step further. One skiff may drop anchor and slack off enough anchor rode to ride comfortably. The other then drops anchor about two boat lengths away from the first in a line perpendicular to the current. Both craft will then be lying some distance apart with the current flowing between them.

Now throw a line from the stern of one boat to the stern of the other. Take up on this line until the sterns are within a foot of each other, and make fast. The turbulence caused by the current flowing by the boats' hulls, which now present a rough V, produces ideal chumming conditions. Shrimp tossed from the bow of each boat will contribute to a wide chum streak that covers a maximum of water. In addition, all embarked anglers can fish without interference, because the whole side of each boat is clear and riding almost perpendicular to the chum slick. This system is not confined to two boats, but may be used for as many as four, simply by anchoring the two outside craft further apart.

One word of caution: never try to bridle boats in this manner if the current is unusually strong or if a brisk wind is blowing. In the excitement of hooking and playing a fish it is all too easy to roll the down-current gunwale under.

As far as individual small boats are concerned, the design for the weakfisherman is primarily a matter of taste, locale—and pocketbook! There's a wide variety to choose from and even the hull materials vary widely, from lapstrake wood to glass fiber, from plywood to aluminum and with an equally wide variation in price.

Basically, the thing to keep in mind when selecting a small boat for weakfishing is the conditions under which the boat will be used most often. Thus, the shallow-draft pirogue of the Louisiana bayou country is ideally suited to waters of that area. Long and lean, this boat can be poled or paddled through narrow passes and over flats that are barely damp.

Such a craft, caught in a squall on Long Island Sound, would survive for a matter of minutes at best. There, the seaworthy, high-sided utility runabout would be a better choice. Stability, rather than the ability to navigate shallows, is the primary requirement on most of the northern fishing grounds.

Similarly, the flat bottomed skiff found at any boat livery from New England to Texas is good enough when fishing grounds are within easy rowing distance in comparatively sheltered waters. This type of craft is inefficient and even dangerous when long distances must be traveled from one fishing ground to the next or when rough seas may be encountered. The seaworthy, fast outboard or small inboard designed for salt water use would be the choice under such conditions.

Do not be misled in the belief that the banks dory, long used by North Atlantic commercial fishermen, is the safest thing afloat for a sportsman. The dory is a magnificent off-shore work boat, at its best when heavily loaded. Lightly loaded—and fishermen are always lightly loaded by comparison with the commercial man—the dory is a cranky, tippy and altogether unsatisfactory craft.

Northern anglers who recognized this fact a great many years ago developed a much more efficient sport fishing hull design in the outboard or Amesbury dory, which features the bow of a standard banks dory, plus a square stern with plenty of bearing surface. This is one of the most seaworthy of small craft and, although it does not lend itself to big motors and high speed, is stable in fairly rough waters.

Progressing north to south, the modern angler will find ever increasing interest in cartop and trailer boats, many of which may be used on the various weakfishing grounds. Practically all of the 12- to 14-foot models which are ordinarily transported on a vehicle's roof rack suffice in sheltered waters, as do the shallow draft trailer boats fitted with outboard motors.

Beach buggy skippers of the North Atlantic coast find that the aluminum boats they use in fishing for surf-running striped bass and bluefish will turn the trick on weakies as well. Major handicap, so far as the aluminum boat is concerned, is the noise factor. Metal water craft resound with every movement of angler and equipment and may often spook wary fish.

However, until fiber glass boat builders are able to produce a craft as light as that made of aluminum, beach buggy anglers will continue to use the featherweight surf skiff. If such a craft is to be used on weakfish, the anglers aboard should consider the affect of noise on this sensitive species. An old army blanket, used underfoot, will absorb a certain amount of unwanted noise; a strip of heavy rug material will do the same. This is particularly important in fishing the northern variety of the *Cynoscion* clan.

Actually, in working the grass flats of Florida's Gulf Coast, we have seen no evidence that the racket produced by a metal boat seriously handicaps seatrout fishing. Where the slap of waves on the side of such a craft will spook bonefish at a considerable distance, spotted seatrout seem oblivious to all but the most exaggerated clamor. Obviously, dropping an anchor on the bottom of an aluminum boat, slamming oars across the thwarts—and otherwise producing unnatural noise—will lessen a fisherman's chances.

Fiber glass and molded plastic boats are excellent choices for the weakfisherman, since their only major handicap (sometimes rightly considered an asset) is greater weight than comparably sized aluminum craft. In the Deep South, there is much to be said for the typical 14- to 18-foot fiber glass boat of Florida's "Back Country." This craft can rocket over miles of shallow bays, yet maneuver quietly when the occasion demands. Most of the medium-sized, outboard-powered fishing boats are transported on trailers. This, in itself, is a testimonial to the resourcefulness of the American boatman.

Well-designed and cleverly fabricated wooden boats are equally effective: in fact, thousands of coastal anglers remain unconvinced that aluminum, glass or the various plastics will ever entirely replace wood as a boat building material. The well-made plywood, planked or lapstrake boat is still the best of its class for a sneak attack on such wary and easily spooked species as the bonefish and the weakie.

As far as large boats are concerned—the charter and party boats of New York and the Chesapeake area are typical—basic design is that of any comparatively shallow draft vessel built to accommodate fish and fishermen. An open cockpit or wide deck space may be unpleasant when the weather is bad, but means ease in handling tackle without interference from boat structure. The cabin cruiser with a small, enclosed cockpit is far from ideal because rarely more than two can fish at the same time and they must fish directly over the transom. In addition, once a fish has been hooked, the angler must duck and dodge to keep his rod clear of obstructions.

A long-handled net, as mentioned previously, is handy wherever the catch must be swung aboard a boat; it is an absolute necessity on a large, high-sided boat. Swinging weakfish over the rail, without benefit of a net, will result in more hook pull-outs than can be imagined in a month of angling nightmares.

No matter what type boat he uses, the smart weakfisherman watches one item in particular. Gunwales, combings, sides and any other portion of the craft that might come in contact with a tight line should be kept as smooth as possible. Light tackle is the rule when a man is chasing the *Cynoscion* family, and any splinter or rough edge that might intercept the line when the quarry dives for shelter under the keel means a lost fish, parted terminal tackle—and a flaming temper on the part of the angler!

This stunt of diving for cover under the boat is a common one for a hooked seatrout. Even a small fish can break up tackle if the angler is not prepared for this startling dash. All too often, the neophyte will react in exactly the wrong manner and will raise his rod tip high in an attempt to check the fish in its run. As a result, terrific strain will be put on the last few inches of the tip—and something is bound to give.

Since a small boat fisherman cannot move his feet to any great degree without joining the fish he has hooked, all he can do is to equalize the strain on his tackle by moving the rod. When the weakfish heads for the keel, the proper and prudent action is to lower the tip—right into the water if necessary—yet still keep the line tight. An arc is thus maintained through the whole length of the rod, even though the fish may actually be swimming behind the angler. It is an uncomfortable situation, at best, and if the critter surfaces on the other side of the boat—prayer, plus a large portion of luck form definite requirements. We have, on several occasions, practically passed a pounding spinning rod under the bow of a boat to keep in touch with a seatrout bent on reversing the field.

Specific tackle for the boat fisherman presents a specialized problem. For example, a standard fly rod will provide maximum sport once a fish has been hooked. However, only an open boat may be used with this tackle, since it is almost impossible to cast if there is any overhead structure. Moreover, the fly rod man will curse any skiff that has slats or duckboards placed over its bottom to keep human feet dry. Loops of shooting line invariably tangle with the ends of such slats at a crucial moment. Moral: if you fish with the light wand and the feather artificial, let your feet get wet and leave the duckboards on the dock.

The foregoing does not apply to the fly rod fisherman who uses nylon monofilament instead of the heavier nylon enameled or treated line. The fly rod monofilament user does not cast a fly, a bait or anything else for any considerable distance: he simply lets his lure stream out in the current. This can be done from any craft that is anchored in the right position.

One specialist that always makes himself unpopular is the light tackle character who makes the mistake of joining a derrick-and-be-damned group aboard a party or small boat. Meat fishermen take a dim view of the spincaster who enjoys the sport of angling so much that he prefers to boat his fish only after a considerable battle. Under such circumstances, the only thing the sport can do is to grin and bear it (crossed lines and parted terminal tackle) and make a mental note never to go out with the heavy tackle boys again.

Boat courtesy, of course, does not stop with those who are actually on board. A mobile boatman obviously should steer clear of beach-bound anglers who may be fishing from a pier, a bridge or even from a particular stretch of shoreline. By the same token, trollers should keep away from still fishermen and drifters. And—the man who cuts through the chum line of a fellow angler deserves to be cut up for chum himself. The oceans of the world are large and there is no reason why a marine hot rodder should conduct his activities in the immediate vicinity of other boat operators.

The golden rule, although it may be considered old fashioned in many quarters today, remains a pretty good guide for the boatman who specializes in catching weakfish.

CHAPTER 7

Right Time—Right Place

ONE FACTOR WHICH HELPS TO SET THE *Cynoscion* TRIBE apart from other sport fish is the extensive range of the species. It would be entirely possible for a determined angler to take a weakfish from the coastal waters of every state bordering the Atlantic Ocean and the Gulf of Mexico. Having done this, the seatrout *aficionado* might then continue a successful quest along the East Coast of Central America.

A stunt of this kind would face difficulty only in Maine and New Hampshire, for, while it is true that weakfish venture into the cold waters of the U.S.—Canadian border area, the species seldom appears there in appreciable numbers. For all practical fishing purposes, Massachusetts marks the northern range boundary, and even that state must be divided. A peak year will find many weakies south of an imaginary dividing line drawn from Provincetown to Plymouth, with few north of the old Pilgrim town.

In those areas which offer the necessary combination of reasonably warm water and abundant bait, the weakfish

114

clan will congregate in certain known areas but will also turn up in locations generally expected to harbor striped bass, bluefish or other sport and game fish. Thus, while a peak season in Massachusetts will find squeteague fishermen focussing their attention on such spots as the Wareham River mouth at Buzzards Bay, big tiderunners will be taken by surf casters seeking striped bass in the Cape Cod Canal, or by squidding enthusiasts working South Cape beaches.

As we mentioned earlier in this book, there is considerable overlapping of range among the various weakfish species. However, a spotted, sand or silver weakfish would be a rarity in Massachusetts, Rhode Island, Connecticut or New York. These relatively cold northern seas play host to the common weakfish only, *Cynoscion regalis*. This is the famed squeteague of Massachusetts and Rhode Island, and the weakfish, weakie or weak of Connecticut and New York.

Regalis may be found almost anywhere in the coastal waters of the north during its cyclic periods of abundance. It does not move into fresh water and is far more sensitive to brackishness than is its southern cousin, the spotted seatrout. Smaller school fish tend to congregate in large groups, while large tiderunners seem to play the lone wolf role.

At this book time, Massachusetts weakfish are almost non-existent. The species exhibits a strange and little-known cycle of scarcity and abundance which follows no set pattern. There is ample evidence that squet will make a comeback along the entire northeast coast.

During a peak year, Bay State anglers take weakfish from a number of locations off Cape Cod and around the southern island chain. There is good fishing in Buzzards Bay and in Massachusetts Bay, plus occasionals in the Cape

Cod Canal. Those who seek this species rely on the grass shrimp chum line, with the same grass shrimp for bait. Some good catches are made on gaudy streamer flies jigged in the chum streaks.

Massachusetts surf casters also account for numbers of king-sized weakies. These fish are hooked on everything from metal squids to midget-plugs and eelskin rigs. They're taken, for the most part, by anglers who are actually fishing for striped bass and blues.

Practically all Bay State weakfishing in the past has been a daytime operation. The return of the species will see little change, although there'll be increased interest in night fishing, particularly in those areas where artificial lights bring small bait swarming to the surface, followed by schools of hungry squeteague.

While Massachusetts anglers enjoy good fishing in the peak years, the sport becomes an obsession in Rhode Island. Narragansett Bay is the key location when squet are plentiful, but fish of all sizes are taken from bays, inlets and surf along the whole, rugged coastline. Nayatt Point in Narragansett Bay is usually recognized as the greatest of all fishing grounds in the state.

Like Massachusetts, Rhode Island prefers to take weakies on grass shrimp in a grass shrimp chum line. Artificial flies and mummichubs are used to a certain extent, as is squid—but the tiny, transparent shrimp of the north are almost indispensable in luring squet. There is little or no fishing with plugs and those fish taken on tinclads are usually strays that muscle into a striped bass or bluefish party.

When the run is on in Narraganset Bay, small skiff chummers find that fishing comes to a grinding halt the moment the sun goes below the horizon. For this reason, many Rhode Islanders are firmly convinced that squeteague will not hit after dark. Such is not the case. Shortly after dark, open water fish apparently take a short vacation, but, by fishing deep and keeping at it, an angler can still entice them. In addition, the larger weaks are apt to start feeding when their smaller brothers loaf. Here, as elsewhere along the coast, artificial lights that attract bait will also attract squet.

Both Massachusetts and Rhode Island find angling at its best in June and July with action continuing through the early fall. Mid-September usually sees the end of good weakfishing, for line storms and rapidly dropping temperatures send the sensitive weakies on their way to warmer climes.

In Rhode Island, the heavy duty fly rod, often mounting a single action reel filled with nylon monofilament, has been and probably will continue to be a popular combination for chum-line fishing. However, thread-line gear will almost certainly be the choice of the majority when squet return in numbers.

Weakfish are making an obvious comeback along the Connecticut shore, where increased catches indicate that old-time angling will soon be equalled or surpassed. Nutmeg State anglers employ the grass shrimp chum line, but here, as elsewhere in the Long Island Sound area, sport fishermen use a variety of lures and baits to tempt their quarry.

Mummichubs, the little brackish water chub that is called "killifish" south of Connecticut, now becomes a major bait. Seaworms are more often employed and serve well behind the flashing blades of a willow leaf or Colorado spinner. Strips of squid tempt big weakies finning in the depths below a chum streak. Flies and small bucktails are successfully employed, almost always in a grass shrimp chum streak. Here, as elsewhere in the northernmost waters of weakfish range, plugs are seldom used and the tin squid is rarely cast for weakies alone.

Connecticut witnesses the arrival of schooling weakfish by mid-May and angling is at its spring best when roses bloom in June. Sport continues through the entire summer, with doldrum periods during the dog days in late July and August. Angling then picks up and remains good until the fish move out in the wake of the first succession of line storms in mid-September or early October.

Weakfish frequent the mouths of the major Connecticut river systems and seem to congregate in the lower end of the Sound around Norwalk. The Housatonic River is an early hot spot and often provides good fishing through the entire summer.

Long Island Sound plays host to big schools of weakies during the same general mid-May to late September season. The recognized hot spots are Peconic, Hempstead and Oyster Bay harbors, but it is well to remember that weakies are scattered along the entire Sound and may be taken in fair to good numbers at any point. Quite often these fish school in company with porgies and are caught on a high-hook, low-hook rig which is used to double an angler's chances when both species are present.

Long Island Sound can necessitate the use of big boats or, at the least, extremely seaworthy small boats. This stretch of water can be rough when angling is at its best, so proper caution should always be observed.

Spinning tackle is almost invariably chosen in this region, but fly rod enthusiasts still fill their fish boxes—and a few ardent souls stick to boat rods and heavy terminal tackle. As in Connecticut, the chum line is employed to a considerable extent, with grass shrimp favored as the tempter. Seaworms and squid, the latter cut in strips, are used to coax big tiderunners, while surf casters squidding the Long Island shore annually account for a number of big yellowfins.

Although there has been little specialized surf fishing for the species in recent years, a surprising number of New Yorkers eschew bass and bluefish, fluke and flounders. to concentrate on weakies. For the most part, these anglers use natural bait and hunt such areas as Jones Beach, Moriches and the Rockaways. When weaks are plentiful, in the peak years, considerable surf casting with small tinclads and bucktails is done. Needless to say, piers and bridges play host to eager throngs of anglers when fish are hitting.

By the first week of June, or even earlier during a warm spring, weakfish appear through the major portion of New York Bay and in the neighboring waters of Sandy Hook and Raritan bays. These early fish feed deep and, when the small boat fleet is operating during a summer weekend, they remain in the depths. Here, the drifter comes into his own and a fluttering strip of squid or a piece cut from a fluke or blowfish belly will outfish the trolled lure two to one. Later, weaks in this area may be taken nearer the surface—but a fleet of boats will invariably force them down.

On the outer shore of New Jersey, along the entire Atlantic Coast of the state, word of a weakfish run triggers a rush to the beaches and a hearty welcome in the form of flying tin squids and bucktails. Although natural bait is favored, particularly during the hot summer months, certain artificials do great execution in the late spring and early fall. The top of the incoming tide is the best bet, except in the vicinity of inlets. There, outgoing currents, which carry bait of all sorts into the ocean, act as a permanent chum line. If weakies are present in numbers, inlet jetties are always lined with anglers armed with everything from heavy surf rods to featherweight spinning sticks.

Big runs of bluefish sometimes spoil weakfishing locations. Since choppers like nothing better than a breakfast of weakies, the two fail to get along peaceably. As an example, the area to the west of Shrewsbury rocks is an excellent spot for weakfish, yet, when big choppers are there in force, it is famed purely and simply as a feeding ground for blues. When the bluefish cycle dips, many one-time weakfish waters will come into their own again.

From Sea Bright, southward along the whole of the North Jersey shore, weakfish are taken in the surf. In this area, small tinclads and bucktails produce catches which range from mediocre to excellent. One of the secrets of success in this clear water section is use of a nylon monofilament leader, rather than wire. Similarly, for bait fishing, a nylon snelled hook is standard equipment. Usually, one short snelled hook is fished low on the rig, while a second, also snelled, is buoyed up by the "Jersey Doodle." Shrimp, seaworms, bits of crab, squid and even sand bugs are used effectively by the bottom fishing legions.

Jetties make excellent platforms for this type of Jersey weakfishing, but piers and bridges should not be neglected. In addition, the canal fishing enthusiast can cast right from the banks of these man-made waterways and is apt to clean up during the fall run.

Moving southward, the traveling angler reaches some of the larger Jersey bays. Barnegat is the first of these, and a name to remember. Here, weakfish arrive in mid-May, during a normal spring, and will often remain until the water becomes so cold in November that they are literally knocked out. In fishing any of these bays, whether drifting or trolling, note that the edges of channels are always promising. In early and late seasons, the deep holes and channels themselves, such as Oyster Creek Channel, produce. But—keep clear of larger craft that may not be interested in fishing!

While currents around the jetties provide a natural chum line, many anglers give nature a hand by tossing grass shrimp off the rocks or over the gunwales of their skiffs. The method also works well around piers and bridges, or anywhere where a current will take the bait out to waiting gamesters. Once a slick has been established, fishing with a squid, a fish belly strip or a bucktail is likely to produce. Surf fishing, incidentally, is good from Seaside Park right down to Barnegat.

Do not neglect the flats in this area: most of the shallow reaches provide good sport for the angler in a poled skiff. The fly rod or the light spinning outfit is indicated. Handicaps include boat traffic that keeps fish off the flats, and weather; at the first sign of a temperature drop, weakies head for deeper water in order to keep their fins from being nipped.

Weakfish assume even greater importance as surf fish along the shores of Long Beach Island. Here, as further north, the two hook rig is preferred, but excellent catches are made on artificials. Fish arrive in mid-May and stay until the line storms of late October or early November warn them to depart. However, the man who is willing to brave a bit of cool weather will catch the heaviest fish. Tiderunners seem to gather along this beach for one last feeding fling before they vanish in the late fall. Evening fishing on the high tide is particularly productive during this period.

On the "inside," in places like the Mullica River, Little Egg Harbor and Great Bay, the man with light tackle and a skiff comes into his own. This is really the outlying fringe of the Jersey "Everglades" country, which is similar in many ways to its Florida counterpart. A sportsman can fish from boat or bank but, from personal experience, we add a word of warning on the latter. Much of the sod bank area is slick under foot and mud holes are plentiful. It is best to take to the land at a known hard spot. Otherwise, on an incoming tide, one may have to slog hip-deep through some of the stickiest mud and mire on the coast. This is not only poor from the fishing point of view, but is downright uncomfortable.

The section west and north of Atlantic City is similar— vast reaches of coastal wilderness with brackish streams meandering between sod banks where fiddler crabs scuttle in and out of their burrows like the trench-bound armies of 1917. In heavily populated New Jersey, these aboriginal backwaters are almost unbelievable. The same word, on occasion, can be used to describe the fishing.

Methods used here can be applied to "swamp weakfishing" anywhere along the coast. The trick is to locate the deep holes and to cast a bucktail or a bait into them. Work the lure across the current for best results. Here, also, a few shrimp dropped into the current as chum may make the difference between success and failure. Finally, pack your mosquito dope: those Jersey eagles, famed in song and story, are particularly robust in the tidal marshes.

Where beaches are available in this southern Jersey area, surfing can be productive. The inlets, such as Absecon, often yield good catches. Small boats may be used on the ocean side around Brigantine and similar stretches, where trolling and drifting are the favored methods. Finally, piers, docks and bridges oblige those who like weakfishing the easy way.

From Ocean City southward, fish arrive during the first weeks of May and some are known to remain through the early winter months. Around Cape May itself, many anglers stick to natural baits. This does not mean that artificials fail to produce, but only that local anglers favor the real McCoy.

Between Jersey and Delaware lie the waters of Delaware Bay, a weakfishing grounds of prime importance over the years. Here drifting, still fishing, chumming and trolling from small boats are productive methods, with casting more popular each year. Magnificent catches are made at Brandywine Shoal, one of the hot spots, and excellent sport is available around the flats on the northern or Jersey side of the bay. Strangely enough, angling pressure in this latter area is comparatively slight.

Pollution has ruined some weakfishing here, but in spite of the filth flowing into the bay out of the Delaware River, weakies seem to survive in surprising numbers. Except in the lower reaches, this is primarily a small boat fishing territory. The bay should also be noted as the first place on the Atlantic Coast where southern spotted weakfish are taken fairly regularly. The specks arrive somewhat later than their common brethren, but depart at much the same time in the fall.

Off Rehoboth Beach and at Indian River Inlet, bucktail casting for weakies has reached a fine art. Here, anglers get a mixed bag of weaks, fluke and striped bass, plus small bluefish in summer and fall. Late season fishing in the deep holes often pays off, with a drifted shrimp or a bucktail bounced along the bottom turning the trick. With the weakfish cycle on the upswing, Delaware Bay should regain its old reputation as a hot spot.

Common weakfish are taken all the way along the seaboard from Ocean City, Maryland, down through the Carolinas, but more of their spotted cousins show in the catch as anglers move southward. Fishing is good on the ocean and bay sides of Assateague Island, and "gray trout" comprise a respectable part of the catch in Chincoteague Bay. There is some shore casting, but the majority of anglers prefer large or small boats. Shrimp and bits of crab are the favored baits, while artificials fall far behind. This is not due so much to the habits of the fish as to the choice of the fishermen. Bait reigns supreme through most of the DelMarVa peninsula..

Just as Delaware Bay marks the overlapping of range in species, the DelMarVa Peninsula may be considered the demarcation line for the so-called clothespin plug. North of the area, although it is becoming more popular, the clothespin is not widely used. Southward, it is a popular lure for both common (gray) and speckled trout.

While the Eastern Shore of Virginia has long been known as a great fishing ground for the common weakfish, southern spotted trout have only recently come into their own in that area. Such angling pioneers as Claude Rogers and Luther Crockett of Virginia Beach have located several highly productive areas and have succeeded in landing numbers of good sized specks. Almost without exception, Rogers, Crockett and their angling companion use artificials. They have opened up a sport which will assume greater importance with each passing year.

On the western side of the Chesapeake, Lynnhaven Inlet and the waters around it are famous for fall runs of seatrout. Here, the man who knows the feeding habits of trout will outfish the neophyte 50 to one. The trick lies in following the fish from bar to bar as the tide advances or recedes. Bucktails and the clothespin plug are the best known lures, with many old timers sticking to the natural shrimp routine.

Quite naturally, the Chesapeake is a fishing world in itself. Mention this huge bay and you speak of the major nursery of the common weakfish of the Atlantic. Other areas have their seasons and locations where fishing is excellent at certain times of the year—but the Chesapeake provides seatrout fishing twelve months on end. Moreover, there are few places in the bay, below Annapolis, where you can go fishing *without* catching weaks!

This may sound like an exaggeration, but it is not. The little cusses swim all over the place and are taken by the thousands in every estuary, on every shoal, in the channels —in fact, everywhere. Naturally, there are times when trout do not bite, but those times are infrequent. Unfortunately, the run of fish in the Chesapeake consists, for the most part, of smaller than average individuals. A glance at the chart of world records prepared by the International Game Fish Association shows not a single record from the Chesapeake in any category. Larger fish are invariably taken from open ocean waters.

So plentiful are the common seatrout, known locally as gray trout, that many local anglers catch them only incidentally while seeking other species. The same anglers will go out of their way to hunt the more highly prized specks. Less particular sportsmen catch thousands of the little gamesters from all sorts of boats, from jetties and sod banks all over and around the bay. To name all of the locations where anglers concentrate would be tantamount to reading a roll call of points, islands, shoals, rivers and bays from Annapolis southward.

Natural bait is the prime catcher in this area, but the atomic age finds more and more sportsmen turning to artificials. Shrimp and bits of crab lead the list in the first named category, while clothespin plugs and bucktails are the choice of casters. Incidentally, nylon and feather or hair lures are included wherever "bucktails" are mentioned: the term is used in the generic sense.

You can take your choice of tackle and methods in the

Chesapeake region—and still be sure of some success. Spinning has made great inroads in the light tackle field, but the users of bait casting gear are still numerous. This is particularly true among pier fishermen who have found that light monofilament has not sufficient strength to derrick catches up from the waters below. Heavier monofilament is often used on orthodox bay and bait casting reels.

South of Cape Henry, to the North Carolina line, there is some surf fishing for weakfish, with speckled seatrout added to the bag in spring and fall. Small boat and pier fishermen take a share of the catch in this area. However, when the sand beaches give way to the marshes of Back Bay, weakfishermen become a minority until the Outer Banks area of North Carolina is reached.

This stretch, which runs from the state line past Cape Hatteras and right down to Cape Lookout, has made an enviable reputation for itself as channel bass country. Note, however, that it also provides good fishing for both of the major weakfishes. Thousands of channel bass fishermen find themselves enjoying hot sessions with specks in the surf.

Natural bait is again favored by surfmen, but any angler who experiments will find that the fish will strike an assortment of bucktails, spoons, clothespin plugs and other lures. Pier and small boat anglers who fish both the ocean and the waters of Currituck, Albemarle, Roanoke, Croatan and Pamlico sounds swear by the clothespin plug and the bucktail. Other lures take fish, but these are favored.

A majority of surfmen use a two hook rig on the bottom, with the low hook (and larger of the two) baited for channel bass. The high riding barb is intended for trout and is usually baited with a shrimp, a piece of crab or a sand bug. As in the Chesapeake area, it would be impossible to name every spot where fish are taken. All of the sounds are nursery areas for both common and spotted trout. As a consequence, small fish are generally taken in the sounds, while larger trout tend to feed on the ocean side or at the mouths of inlets.

So far as boat fishing is concerned, drifting, still fishing and casting are preferred—with trolling a poor fourth. Like the area slightly to the north, spring and fall provides the best sport with specks, while common weakfish are hooked throughout the year. Skiff poling is practically unknown in this region, but our personal experience indicates that it can be highly effective on the flats in the various sounds, particularly in the hours of early evening.

By the time Core Sound and Cape Lookout are reached, speckled trout take over from the gray or common variety, both in numbers and in popularity. Fishing methods and seasons are similar but there is a trend toward the use of artificial lures in the surf. And, because certain lures have proved effective, natural bait fishing is on the decline. More and more fishermen are turning to light tackle casting—and they are accounting for big strings of fish.

Boat liveries and piers are plentiful in the general area of Beaufort and Morehead City, with the result that trout fishing is a major sport. The fall run of specks in the various river estuaries and in the eastern end of Bogue Sound is particularly good. As elsewhere along this whole coast, a storm will roil the shallow sound waters and fishing will suffer for a few days thereafter. It is always wise to keep a sharp eye on the weather reports when planning a trip.

Southeastern North Carolina—in general the Onslow Bay section—provides excellent trout fishing. The best run of fish appears during the first week of November and good catches are made through the first of the year. Trout remain in many of the deep holes through the entire winter season. When cold weather touches the coast, some of these late-run fish are caught on the shallows and suffer from what the natives call "trout numb." This is no more or less than the stunned condition reported earlier in this volume, but the term is particularly descriptive. Fish remain alive, but lose the power of motion to a large degree and may be caught by the simple process of picking them up.

In this section, the ardent seatrout angler is generally equipped with a small, but seaworthy outboard-powered boat, waders and a light casting rig of either the fixed spool or bait casting type. He hunts his fish along the open beaches, in the bays and in the sounds, often anchoring his craft or pulling it high and dry on a bar while he wades and casts to promising sloughs and holes. A newcomer to the area should secure the services of a guide, for the change in currents at every stage of the tide can only be learned by long experience.

At this point on the coast, the type of lure used with greatest success also undergoes change. One of the favorites is the small, red and white MirrOlure. Such specialists as Dan Holt fish it with deadly effectiveness, allowing the plug to sink briefly and then retrieving it rather slowly with accompanying jerks of the rod tip. The strike is apt to come immediately after the rod tip is twitched.

In addition to the seatrout specialists—and there are many—an army of pier and bridge fishermen work the coast. These anglers favor artificials but, in the early season, bait may be the only successful offering. Shrimp and crabs are again the favorites. Small boat still fishermen and drifters take a share of trout, as do surfmen. Surf casters, if they are seeking trout alone, favor the light tackle of the specialists.

Winter fishing for resident specks is done to a large extent with natural bait, and local knowledge is a necessity since the angler must anchor above a hole and drift his bait into its depths. On warm winter days it is possible to make a killing in this manner, but few practice it, simply because it is uncomfortable sport at best—and downright dangerous if a sudden storm arrives on the scene.

Surf fishing is the primary method of taking trout in the northern section of South Carolina and, oddly enough, the anglers generally forsake artificial lures and return to natural bait. The big rods of the more northern areas are again in evidence at Little River, Myrtle Beach, Murrell's Inlet and down to Winyah Bay. Exceptions are found among a few skiff fishermen and a vast horde of folk who pursue their sport from the piers. These anglers use clothespin plugs, bucktail type lures and a scattering of sub-surface plugs. The season is similar to that of southeastern North Carolina, but the lack of sounds and bays precludes extensive winter fishing.

Angling pressure from Winyah Bay southward through the many small islands in the Bulls Bay area is light, but the success ratio is high. Here, a skiff fisherman trolling, still fishing, casting or drifting will do well. Although chumming seems to be an unknown art south of the Virginia Capes, it can be used with great success. The many channels, holes and sloughs provide natural feeding grounds and an angler anchored up-current from them should be able to entice trout.

Charleston, at the mouth of the Cooper and Ashley rivers, is a population center and trout fishermen are much in evidence. Launching small outboards in the surf—and the surf is usually mild when fishing is good—is a common practice along all of the outer islands and from the mainland itself. Seatrout anglers do considerable trolling along the bars and at the breakwaters off Charleston. Good catches are also made right from the sea wall running along the Battery and at other points in the city proper.

Anglers are about evenly divided between those who cast artificials and those who still fish with bait. Many embrace both methods with outstanding success. During the fall run, particularly, casters outfish bottom bouncers. In the heat of summer, the natural article works best.

Local specialists in this area do a great deal of winter trout fishing, with the most productive period occurring during October, November and early December. Seatrout are concentrated in the brackish creeks at this time, sometimes in astonishing numbers. Spinning tackle is employed by the faithful, together with quarter-ounce bucktail jigs or live shrimp. Late fall and winter creek fishing can be uncomfortable, for the weather is often raw. It can also be exceptionally productive. These specialists often fish commercially, selling their catch.

Creek fishermen who use the bucktail favor a cast across the current and a slow, bumping retrieve along the bottom. As the season progresses and trout are chilled by low water temperatures, the strike is very light and it takes an alert angler to set the hook. During December's full moon period, night fishermen sometimes account for big specks with plastic sub-surface plugs of the reflector type. These lures are worked slowly, twitched along just under the surface, and often lure heavyweights out of the depths.

A rising or falling tide, rather than full flood or dead low, is favored. Since success in angling trout in the brackish streams depends, for the most part, on knowledge of currents, bottom conformation and bait movement, the newcomer to the area should always essay his sport in the company of a local expert.

Further south, the coast is broken up into many islands, bays, rivers and inlets. Pier fishermen take advantage of the ocean front, but almost all other trout addicts play inland waters. Trolling with a feather, nylon jig or small spoon pays off in locating schools which may then be punished through the casting and drifting techniques. For those who desire to fish from shore, the banks of the inland waterway route are suggested. There are many access areas to this ship channel.

One thing that should be remembered about the Edisto —Saint Helena—Beaufort—Port Royal areas: a light wire leader is practically a necessity when fishing. The reason is obvious when you examine the bottom conformation: a vast number of oysters rise like stalagmites from the ocean floor, each sharp enough to cut a taut line. Trout seem to realize that such obstructions are their friends; once hooked they dash for cover. Lacking the protection offered by a fairly long leader, the angler will lose a succession of fish—and lures.

The area is not heavily fished, but it is a genuine paradise for the seatrout enthusiast. Not only are specks here in numbers, but they are present through the entire year. An angling native may be difficult to locate but, once located, he should be cultivated. Such a man can save a great deal of unrewarding exploration and lead the way to the hot spots.

Georgia's salt and brackish water coastline is roughly similar to that found in southern South Carolina, but the numbers of tidal rivers and creeks are even greater. This is excellent seatrout country and the species affords sport to at least 80 percent of the anglers in that area. The spotted variety is known locally as "winter trout" and is caught from October through March, with peak fishing in November, December and January. Common weakfish, known as "summer trout," are present all year, with particularly good runs during the spring and fall.

Although surf fishing with heavy tackle accounts for many fish, they are usually taken on such gear incidentally while fishing for some of the heavyweights, such as channel bass. A far more efficient outfit is the spinning rod or bait casting combination. The angler may wade the countless flats, beaches and channel edges, cast into the holes and sloughs and find sport second to none. There are also numerous fishing piers for those who like to keep their feet dry.

For the most part, ocean side beaches are sandy and hard, which means wading and casting is easy. On the land side, silt from the rivers tend to make the bottom soft and a small boat is an asset. The Georgia coast is a fascinating area to explore and the fishing possibilities are just beginning to be realized.

As might be suspected, major fishing effort is expended around the population centers. Savannah in the north and Brunswick in the south, the latter with its neighboring resort sections at St. Simon and Sea Island, are the spots where seatrout fishermen gather. The many channels and bridges accessible to the sportsman who owns a car, the winding, brackish creeks that forever invite a boatman to investigate "the next bend," all offer good trout fishing.

Although artificials are used throughout Georgia, natural bait is favored because fishermen are generally seeking bottom feeders as well as trout. Cane poles are much in evidence here, but thousands of local and visiting anglers are equipped with spinning and bait casting gear. Shrimp is the major bait, with bits of crab second in importance. Here, as in South Carolina, exploration with a skiff pays off, particularly in the late fall. Again, for the bank fisherman, the inland waterway channel is an excellent starting point.

All of the various weakfish, with the possible exception

of the little sand seatrout of the Gulf, appear on Florida's East Coast. Yet, while runs of common weakies are regularly reported in the deep bays and channels from Jacksonville south through the Indian River country and even to the Keys, the southern spotted seatrout is the species of greatest single importance. *Cynoscion nebulosus* is the trout of the South, a sport fish that obliges all hands from Jacksonville to the Keys and north to the Panhandle.

Northeast Florida fishermen account for tons of these fighters during each calendar year, taking them from the surf, the creeks, the flats, the rivers and the inland waterways. Weaks are present throughout the year but are most plentiful and obliging in the cool weather months, particularly in spring and fall. At these seasons, trout are changing their feeding grounds and are snapping up a variety of live baits.

Anglers in the Jacksonville area take magnificent catches at the mouth of the St. Johns River and from the inland waterway. Jetties and piers jutting out into the Atlantic also yield strings of fish. Angling is at its best in spring and fall when a light woolen shirt feels comfortable. Winter fishermen use shrimp and bucktail lures to probe for and to haul trout out of the deep holes in brackish inland waters.

Somewhat further south, in the fabulous Indian River country, trout are taken throughout the year, with spring, fall and winter producing best catches. Anglers of this section prefer spinning and bait casting tackle to other combinations—and threadline is favored. The purists swear by bucktails and sub-surface plugs like the MirrOlure and Needlefish, but surface poppers also produce good catches. Dawn is considered to be the best fishing period, with late afternoon a close second. Either time is enhanced by an outgoing tide and bottom conformation that features a sudden drop-off. Boat fishermen who operate during the mid-winter months catch hundreds of trout by bouncing well-weighted shrimp into the deep holes of channels and creeks. Chumming is almost unknown because local sportsmen feel that they can always locate schools of fish.

Discuss seatrout with a Floridian of the Indian River country and you will come away convinced that this is the world's greatest stamping ground of the species. Gulf Coast enthusiasts may smile scornfully, but it is quite true that the warm, inland sea called the Indian River produces some of the world's heaviest southern weakfish. Moreover, this section is a consistent producer of heavyweights.

Fishing can be spectacular all the way from Cape Canaveral down through the St. Lucie Inlet at Stuart. Cocoa, Eau Gallie, Melbourne, Sebastian Inlet, Ft. Pierce, Jensen Beach, Stuart and Salerno all contribute to a legend that is based on the record of many successful years. Cocoa, just south of Cape Canaveral, calls itself "Seatrout Capitol of the World" and it is a fact that the surrounding Indian River, Banana River, Barge Canal and Canaveral Harbor are among the greatest seatrout fishing grounds found on any coast. Fishing is good throughout the year but reaches its peak in spring and fall.

Seatrout are available along the entire length of Florida's East Coast: thousands of the spotted, silvery gamesters are taken from Miami sea walls and from the multitude of bridges that lace the state's myriad waterways from Jacksonville to Key West. Spinning, bait casting tackle and the time-honored cane pole are most often employed on this seaboard. The traditional popping rod, cork and live shrimp combination is also used, but this outfit is more at home on the Gulf of Mexico.

Many thousands of seatrout are taken from the crystal waters of the Keys, both from the bridges and from the extensive flats, during the course of a year. Yet, when a South Florida angler thinks about frying-size trout, he generally pictures the Southwest Gulf Coast. The Cape Sable area is a recognized hot spot, with vast grass flats and shell bars providing a banquet table for immense schools of fish. The peak season is late winter and early spring when the iridescent scrappers are concentrated close to shore. During the summer months these fish move into deeper water but may still be taken in good numbers. Again, during the late fall, angling reaches fever pitch. Fish are usually available in the brackish creeks of the area during the mid-winter period.

Practically all of the bays, inlets and creeks that break up the mangrove-studded Gulf Coast of Florida are alive with trout at specific seasons. Spring and fall produce the better catches, but there is seldom a week of absolute doldrums. Grass flats and shell bars are the prime fishing grounds in spring and fall, together with the mouths of streams and the deep holes and channels when very hot— or very cold—weather touches the coast.

The traveling angler who works the great, unexploited Northwest Coast of Florida soon learns that the seatrout is first in the affection of the angling majority. Piers, bridges and small boats are the favored fishing platforms, and shrimp is the number one bait. There is less emphasis on artificial lures in this region, although spin and bait casters often prove the worth of manufactured tempters by filling their boats with trout. The popping rod with cork float and shrimp—and the cane pole—are increasingly evident as you move north and west.

This is seatrout country with a vengeance, a beneficent vengeance that brings tens of thousands of men, women and children to the grass flats and the shell bars, the brackish creeks and the mouths of rivers for no other reason than to fish for trout. Many of the rivers on this wild and beautiful seaboard bear Indian names, yet they are synonymous with silvery, speckled trout. Such streams as the Caloosahatchee, Chassahowitzka, Homosassa, Crystal, Suwanee and Steinhatchee are exceedingly kind to sport fishermen.

It's a vast and beautiful area, sometimes hard to reach and rarely exploited after the manner of Florida's famed "Gold Coast." One finds immense grass flats, like those lying in the shelter of Tampa Bay; an abundance of bridges, each catering to thousands of anglers each year; streams pouring their clear, brackish tides into the Gulf. And bays, inlets, flats innumerable.

Here, depending upon weather conditions, the spring run gets under way during the last weeks of February. If lower than average temperatures prevail, fish remain in the streams. Granted sudden warmth, they venture out on the grass flats. By March, trout are almost always out of the rivers, feeding on the inshore flats. There's a great deal of movement at this time, for third month is a changeover period. Even in a land of mockingbirds and palms, the vernal equinox is obvious on earth and sea.

April, May and early June fishing is exceptionally good on the inshore grounds. Thereafter, rising water temperatures cause a mass migration to deeper water. Although trout are still taken in fair to good numbers from piers, bridges and small boats, the furious action of April and May will not be repeated until cooler weather arrives in the fall. Late in September, and during October, specks begin their shoreward movement, usually right on the heels (or flippers) of hordes of shrimp flitting toward their spawning grounds in coastal bays and rivers. A second blitz fishing period gets under way at this time and continues through most of November. Inshore trolling, casting and drift fishing all pay off. By December, resident specks are back in the deep holes of coastal streams where they may be taken in fair to good numbers through the remainder of the winter.

Seatrout of this Northwest Coast of Florida average one to two pounds apiece. A five-pounder is considered something of a heavyweight and, although larger specks are taken, a sportsman should not expect to find the so-called "gator trout" of the Indian River Country on this seaboard. As compensation, Gulf seatrout populations vastly outnumber those of the East Coast.

Logically enough, Alabama, Mississippi, Louisiana and Texas seasons are similar to those of Florida's Northwest Gulf. There is the same early spring movement out of inland waters, and a corresponding migration back to the shallows in the fall. Spring and fall are the peak fishing periods, but angling is a year around proposition.

While the trout of Northwest Florida feel the urge to migrate by late February, Alabama's specks seldom move out of inland waters prior to March. February, here, is an in-between season. Action is spotty, with best catches reported from the deep holes of inland streams and bays. By the first week of March, trout begin to move, but fishing remains erratic. Fastest action is reserved for the estuaries and river mouths. Later, specks leave the rivers and appear in more open waters. By the last two weeks in March an angler may expect fair to good fishing in Mobile and Bon Secour bays. Artificials are employed, but those who seek big trout bait with small croakers, finger mullet and shrimp.

Offshore fishing gets under way in April when the grass flats and oyster beds play host to great schools of trout. Specks are more plentiful at the river mouths and inlets. By May, the peak of the spring season is close at hand. Fish are scattered through brackish water and salt, with specks and whites along the coast and in the inlets. Skiff fishing is good in Mobile and Bon Secour bays—and most of the boatmen employ live shrimp, small mullet and spot for bait. Bits of blue crab often take big catches in the bayous. Casting, trolling and still fishing all account for trout at this time. Surf fishing is practiced to a certain extent, while piers and bridges are payoff locations.

As in Florida, the grass flats and shell beds provide excellent sport during the month of June. As temperatures rise, during July and August, fish move offshore. There are, however, always a certain number of them available on the flats and in the deeper bay locations. Anglers find white (silver) trout in the depths, with specks on the grass beds and oyster reefs. Mid-summer angling is fair to good, but action picks up with the month of September. During this early fall period, specks and white trout are somewhat larger than they were in the spring—and white trout often weigh more than their spotted cousins, particularly in Mobile and Bon Secour bays. The largest specks are caught at night.

From mid-September through the entire month of November, fall fishing reaches its peak in Alabama waters. Specks move into the streams and the Intracoastal Canal by October and fish are scattered through all of the streams of the Mobile River Delta. Hot spots are the Fish, Magnolia, Bon Secour rivers; the streams of Perdido and Wolf bays, and innumerable waters above the Mobile Causeway. November is one of the great fishing months in this area— and trolling is the favored technique. Fast action begins with the first cool weather of autumn and continues right through December, often to the first of the year. Specks strike best from the first streak of dawn to full daylight, and again in the evening and night hours. An outgoing tide is preferred by the specialists.

The same general seasons apply in Mississippi's salt and brackish waters. Seatrout fishing is at low ebb in February, but shows improvement with the first spell of warm weather in March. By the end of this third month, specks begin to leave coastal streams for their spawning grounds in bay and offshore waters. Location of schools is uncertain at this time, due to continuous movement. On-again, off-again sport is the rule in bayous and rivers.

April witnesses a mass movement of specks—out of the rivers and into bays and inlets. Speckled trout fishing in the sound is vastly improved by mid-month, while white trout begin to hit baits and artificials. Petit Bois Pass often provides excellent fishing at this time, with speckled trout the quarry. Live shrimp is the major tempter, but artificials are also used by casters and trollers.

May ushers in the peak of the spring season on Mississippi Sound. White trout are found in almost all bay waters and specks are plentiful on the grass flats and oyster reefs. Trout fishing is excellent at Biloxie and Bay St. Louis, and at the oyster reefs off Pass Christian. Most of the favored spots produce during May and June. Then, in July, there's a summer peak which finds anglers paying strict attention to the channels and comparatively deep oyster beds where trout congregate.

Warm weather in August confines fish to bay and Gulf waters, but fishing remains fair to good. Seatrout please bridge and pier fishermen using everything from the latest light spinning tackle to cane poles, while skiff fishermen enjoy fast action over the oyster beds and channels. Once again, September witnesses the beginning of a fall movement toward shore. Angling is exceptionally good in bay waters and inside coastal areas and it gets better with each passing week. During October there's a general movement toward coastal streams—but one that fluctuates with each weather change. A cold spell, for example, triggers fast fishing at the mouths of streams, while warm weather sends fish back to the flats.

Peak fishing in the fall occurs in November. Specks move into all of the tidal streams and inland waters, but bay and Gulf areas continue to produce. Trolling with artificial lures is favored at this time, but casting and still fishing are practiced by thousands of anglers. Live shrimp, small croakers and minnows are the preferred baits. From November through January, the traveling angler should pay strict attention to such hot spots as the Tchouticabouffa, Jordan, Biloxie and Wolf rivers; Bayou Binas Choire, Bayou Arcadia, Bayou Portage, Bayou Bernard and Fort Bayou. Many tidal streams yield big catches of specks.

Louisiana's coastal pattern is little changed from that of Alabama and Mississippi. With few exceptions, February trout fishing is confined to brackish streams where anglers still fish with bait. One exception: some of the largest specks of the year are regularly taken at Lake Ponchartrain during this second month of the year. The south shore of the vast, marine lake, in the vicinity of Irish Bay, has always been a promising spot. Ponchartrain should be noted among the great weakfishing centers of the coast, for it provides fast action during most months of the year. Even in March, when most specks are leaving inland waters for their summer feeding grounds in the bays and open Gulf, this huge stretch of water north of New Orleans provides fine fishing.

All along the Louisiana Coast, spring fishing perks in April and reaches its peak in May. The offshore oil rigs are favored locations from late April through the summer months. There, fishing is good day and night with night sport most fascinating to the visitor. Swarms of bait fish are attracted by the flare from burning waste materials and vast schools of seatrout rush the hypnotized, unhappy bait. Louisiana sportsmen swear by artificial lures and use them in many areas. Plugs and spoons take fine hauls of specks at Plaquemines Parish Canal. Plugs trolled deep along Lake Ponchartrain trestles snag heavy fish. Spinning with nylon jigs is productive around Grand Isle, primarily for silver trout. Live shrimp and small bait fish are equally popular, accounting for outstanding catches.

September, once again, finds trout moving toward the shore and their winter habitat. They generally reach the inlets late in the month, at the time that fall storms produce silt and darkened water. Weather is often the major deterrent to good fishing during this period. In October and November, brackish lakes Borne and Ponchartrain, opening on Mississippi Sound, are trout fishing hot spots. Specks are particularly plentiful in Ponchartrain, but Grand Lake opening, further west, is favored by many. However, the former is Louisiana's leading inland trout fishing location.

Although fish are moving inland by the last week of September, sport does not end around the offshore oil rigs. Flare fishing remains good right through the first weeks of November, day and night. This is a new thrill for a legion of anglers and one that will become more popular in the future.

May and October are the peak seasons in Texas, with angling fair to good at any time of the year. Trout exhibit the usual southern migrational pattern: out of inland waters during the early spring and back to the shelter of brackish water in the fall. There is considerable bay and flats fishing, plus oil rig fishing in the Galveston Bay area.

Shrimp, as elsewhere on the Gulf, are the major tempters—but Texas anglers are conscious of the artificial lure. Spoons, bucktails and plugs are used along the entire coast.

Here, also, one is most likely to make the acquaintance of the true Gulf Coast popping rod. The outfit has been modernized by many: instead of a cane pole or split bamboo popping rod and service reel, anglers use spinning or medium weight orthodox bait casting gear. The cork float, placed about two feet ahead of a long shanked hook which is baited with shrimp, remains unchanged. It is difficult to describe the thrill of casting this rig to a promising slough, or to a slick on the surface of the water: pop the cork, wait a moment and—wham! Make no mistake, the popping cork rig is deadly on seatrout.

Much wading is done by anglers along the Texas Coast, for the water shoals gradually. Specialists move slowly, shuffling their feet along the bottom to flush occasional sting rays, and halting often to make casts to likely looking holes or to slicks which indicate the presence of trout. Light tackle is invariably employed and terminal gear ranges from the popping cork and shrimp to small plastic plugs. These, incidentally, are murderous when trout are found chasing finger mullet.

The wading angler tries to be on his chosen location before dawn, so that he can fish the potent period of daybreak. He also tries to fish an area which is sheltered from the wind—since wind will roil shallow water and make impossible the stalking of fish. Specks feed close to the shore during the night hours. Then, when the east begins to brighten, these gamesters slowly move toward the depths, feeding as they go.

In spite of the presence of great game fish offshore, channel bass, cobia, black drum and other scrappers within easy reach, the seatrout is the most popular sport fish in Texas.

Whether fishing in the hell-red light from an offshore oil
rig's gas flare, from a party boat in Corpus Christi Bay,
from a fast runabout criss-crossing Laguna Madre—or from
any of the sloping Gulf beaches—the angler of the Lone
Star State is pleased when he finds trout.

Laguna Madre is another of the great locations that
must be mentioned together with Narragansett Bay in
Rhode Island; Long Island's Peconic Bay; Lynnhaven Inlet on the western side of the Chesapeake Bay, and the
Indian River on Florida's East Coast. Madre, in southern
Texas, is a hot spot that draws anglers from every state in
the union—and the trout is number one on the list of de-
sirable gamesters.

Laguna Madre is shallow, often roiled by winds that stir
the mud bottom. It features vast grass flats that line the
shores around spoil bank islands, and by channels that act
as concentration points for trout when they are loafing or
have been forced into the depths by cool weather. Anglers
of this area use a great many artificial lures—and live
shrimp—to catch specks. The popping cork rig is employed
by a sizable majority, but there is evidence that spinning
and plug casting will soon dominate. Small, chrome plated
spoons, together with popping and sub-surface mirror plugs
do great execution.

Sportsmen who fish Laguna Madre are using boats similar to those employed in South Florida—14- to 18-foot glass
or wooden runabouts powered by big outboard motors.
These craft are capable of covering great distances in a
minimum of running time, yet draw so little water that
they are ideal fishing platforms on the flats. Here, as in
Florida, individual trout—or schools of trout—are stalked.
The fish are sometimes betrayed by the presence of birds,
and often spotted through the tell-tale streak of coffee-
colored mud they leave behind them as they swim. Once

in position to reach these gamesters, anglers cast plugs or spoons—which are then retrieved in short flicks of the wrist. The specialists often return to their docks with magnificent catches.

The long coast of Texas plays host to armies of seatrout fishermen during the course of each year and, since the angler has more than 350 miles of seaboard to fish, he can choose the most promising location—even the best weather pattern. Party and private craft compete in a never-ending search for fish. Pier, bridge and jetty jockeys take a full share. Spotted, silver and sand seatrout are found all the way from the Louisiana border down through Port Isabel to the Rio Grande. All three species are taken in numbers but the spotted variety, as elsewhere in the South, is the major quarry.

South of the Mexican border, weakfish decline in numbers, yet there is ample evidence that the species is represented along the coasts of Central America. Similarly, several kissin' cousins, notably the white sea bass, are found on the Pacific coast. Basically, though, the four seatrout (or weakfish) discussed in this book are fish of the salt and brackish seaboards of the Eastern United States. They are the game fish of the multitudes, beloved of tens of thousands, perhaps millions, of everyday sport fishermen from New England to Texas. That alone is worthy accolade to the silvery, iridescent little battler that has, for so many years, belied its given name.

Index